INSTRUCTOR'S MANUAL
AVAILABLE

EXPLORATIONS IN SOCIAL RESEARCH:

Qualitative and Quantitative Applications

Jeanne Kohl

University of Washington

Jane Reisman

Pacific Lutheran University
Organizational Research Services

ROXBURY PUBLISHING COMPANY

NOTE TO INSTRUCTORS:

A comprehensive **Instructor's Manual/Answer Guide** is available from the publisher on request.

Library of Congress Cataloging-in-Publication Data

Kohl, Jeanne, 1942–
    Explorations in social research: qualitative and quantitative
    applications / Jeanne Kohl, Jane Reisman.
        p. cm
    Includes bibliographical references and index.
    ISBN 0-935732-33-0
        1. Social sciences—Research—Methodology.   I. Reisman, Jane
    II. Title
H61.K649   1993   93-21681
300'.72—dc20   CIP

EXPLORATIONS IN SOCIAL RESEARCH: QUALITATIVE AND QUANTITATIVE APPLICATIONS

Publisher: Claude Teweles
Editors: Ingrid Herman Reese, Claude Teweles, Anton Diether
Assistant Editor: Dawn VanDercreek
Cover Design: Allan Miller
Typesetting and Design: Ingrid Herman Reese

Printed in the United States of America on acid-free paper

ISBN 0-935732-33-0

ROXBURY PUBLISHING COMPANY
P.O. Box 491044
Los Angeles, California 90049
(213) 653-1068

Table of Contents

Quick-Glance Subject Index

TOPIC	CHAPTER

Acknowledgements

We would like to acknowledge our appreciation to three individuals who provided assistance to us in the preparation of our book: Patrice Carrello who assisted in arranging and conducting the interviews; Linda Stevens who assisted in preparing the glossary; and Susan McGinty who assisted in editing.

Thanks also go to Al Goodyear, who was instrumental in the development of this book and who provided many helpful insights, including the idea of including guest interviews.

We especially appreciate the contributions of the social researchers interviewed for this book who so candidly and generously shared their experiences and views with us.

We would also like to acknowledge our appreciation to the reviewers of our manuscript at various stages of preparation and revision, including the following whose names are known to us:

> Kenneth Bollen, University of North Carolina at Chapel Hill
> Sheila Cordray, Oregon State University
> David L. Decker, California State University, San Bernardino
> Patrick Donnelly, University of Dayton
> Kenneth Eckhardt, University of Delaware
> Susan Garfin, Sonoma State University
> Sandra K. Gill, Gettysburg College
> David Nasatir, California State University, Dominguez Hills
> James C. Peterson, Western Michigan University
> Josephine A. Ruggiero, Providence College
> William F. Skinner, University of Kentucky
> Bruce Wiegand, University of Wisconsin at Whitewater
> Richard A. Wright, University of Scranton

Our special appreciation goes to Claude Teweles, the publisher at Roxbury Publishing Company, who initiated the concept of the book and worked with us throughout the entire project, providing both encouragement and resources. His editorial staff, too, deserve our thanks for their attention to the "readability" factor.

Lastly, but importantly, we extend our greatest appreciation to our families for offering support and the time to work on the book and the consequent time spent apart from family members: Jeanne Kohl's spouse Alex Welles and their children, Randall, Brennan, Terra, Kyle, and Devon, as well as her mother, Elizabeth Kohl, and brother, Terry Kohl; Jane Reisman's spouse Jay Soroka and children, Audrey and Stevie.

Preface for Instructors

Explorations in Social Research: Qualitative and Quantitative Applications offers students the opportunity for a closer involvement with the research process than they are likely to achieve with only a standard research methods text at their disposal.

This book offers real-life research examples and exercises, which allow students to participate directly in research situations. This *active-learning approach* of actually *doing* research will help them experience first-hand the challenges, choices, and rewards of conducting research.

Each chapter consists of three sections: *Research Briefs*, *Tools and Data*, and *Applications*.

Research Briefs

The Research Briefs are concise summaries of studies that illustrate various research topics and approaches. They present challenges typically encountered in research situations and show how researchers have overcome these challenges. Each Research Brief is followed by assessment questions to help students examine their understanding of the material and to engage them in *critical thought processes*. Both multiple-choice and short-answer questions are provided to accommodate various instructional styles. They can be used as the basis for class discussion or graded assignments.

Tools and Data

The Tools and Data sections focus on the "nuts and bolts" of research. They illustrate the use of various research tools, such as data collection instruments, questionnaire items, and requests for proposals. The data provided include field notes, statistical tables, and interview excerpts from original or fictional sources. The accompanying assessment questions help to fortify student comprehension and provide an opportunity to work with different types of tools and data.

Applications

The Applications are mini-projects which allow students to carry out and then evaluate research activities. They are each designed to be completed in a week or less. The project-oriented approach of these applications supplies a dynamic learning tool.

Interviews with prominent social researchers are included in Chapter 16, followed by exercises and discussion questions. The interviewees are asked what drew them to the field of social research, how they went about choosing research topics, what were their greatest research challenges, and how they dealt with them. These interviews personalize the research process by giving students an inside view of a researcher's personal experiences.

Flexible, Accessible Format

Although the body of knowledge in social research methods texts has become fairly standardized, the order of presentation and emphasis of each text often varies. Individual instructors will find it easy to adapt *Explorations in Social Research* to their needs because the chapters and sections are self-contained units. They can assign chapters in any order or utilize sections of chapters, according to the design and emphasis of their own courses.

Explorations in Social Research also covers various types of research. In addition to quantitative and "basic" research studies, it includes many examples of both *qualitative* and *applied research*. This approach allows instructors to provide a broad introduction to the social research field or to be selective in their emphasis. Furthermore, the text integrates *gender, race, social class, and ethnicity* as it explores such areas as research topics, research variables, and research populations.

Another important feature of this book is its *unifying framework*—which will help to ground student analysis of research decisions. This framework focuses attention on three important challenges within the research process, as discussed in Chapter One: the influence of bias, the effect of research on human subjects, and the contrast between scientific and common-sense orientations.

Finally, this book has been designed to be accessible to students. Its conversational writing style will help to break down some of the learning barriers so common among students taking this course. The perforated, easily removable pages for exercise questions provide a convenient way for students to submit assignments.

Suggested answers to all assessment questions are listed in the accompanying *Instructor's Manual*.

To the Student

Explorations in Social Research: Qualitative and Quantitative Applications offers real-life research examples and exercises. This book will facilitate your discovery of the exciting and complex challenges involved in the research process.

The book offers several distinctive features. First, you will find discussion throughout the book of three sub-themes: the influence of bias, working with human subjects, and the contrast between scientific orientation and common sense. Discussed in the first chapter, they represent major challenges which can affect all aspects of the research process.

Second, the book includes exercises based on the real-life challenges of typical research. The Research Briefs, Tools and Data, and Applications (mini-projects) may be used by your instructor as in-class exercises and/or as out-of-class assignments. The Research Briefs are concise summaries of approaches and decisions found in actual research; they are accompanied by a series of assessment questions for you to answer. The Tools and Data sections are drawn from either original or fictional studies and are accompanied by a series of assessment questions. The Applications are activities to be conducted by you. Assessment questions follow.

Third, Chapter 16 of the book presents short interviews with well-known and highly regarded sociologists and other social science researchers. They answer questions about their experiences and views. We hope this chapter will provide you with additional insights into how research is conducted—how people select topics to study, how their interests change or develop over time, the challenges they face, and the ways in which they deal with them. This personalized view of the field is not typically available in standard research texts.

Fourth, the book is very readable and offers a variety of problems being researched, approaches to conducting research, and relevant assignments. We tried to select examples that would not duplicate those found in standard texts.

Finally, the book reflects a focus on diversity and cross-sectional representation based on gender, race, ethnicity, and social class. Research and researchers are not limited to certain segments of society. Thus, *Explorations in Social Research* reflects the variety and diversity which exist in the world of research, as well as the special challenges involved in conducting research with different population groups.

We hope you find the book useful, instructive, and enjoyable.

Copyright Acknowledgements

Chapter 1

The World of Research

✔ *Are You Ready for the Challenge of Becoming a Researcher?*

✔ *Bias*

✔ *Human Subjects*

✔ *Common Sense*

Chapter 1

The World of Research

Are You Ready for the Challenge of Becoming a Researcher?

Congratulations! You have just been selected out of a competitive pool of applicants for a research internship with Results, Inc. This is an exciting opportunity, which will offer you opportunities for challenge, responsibility, decision making, discovery, and, perhaps, even fame and fortune. We urge you to give this offer serious consideration. Perhaps it would help if we told you more about the position.

You will be conducting social research. Your scope of inquiry will be as expansive as your imagination will allow, the possibilities for engaging your creative powers— limitless.

Social research will increase your involvement in and knowledge about society. Researchers set out to describe social settings, explore issues, and measure attitudes and beliefs. They test hypotheses by asking questions, making direct observations, and studying existing materials. Through careful examination of the data they gather, they detect systematic patterns in attitudes, behavior, beliefs, skills, and so on. Awareness of these patterns adds to our understanding of social organization, which can lead to important decisions related to policies and practices. Furthermore, research skills serve as a significant asset in a variety of career fields, including marketing, communications, administration, human resources, and social services. The ability to conduct surveys and interviews or to analyze databases can be an important aspect of many jobs.

Before you make a decision about this research internship, you should acquire some firsthand experience. In using this book, you will be directly involved in the research process and discover, through active participation, the types of challenges and decisions that engage the social researcher.

Each chapter of this book is divided into three sections: *Research Briefs, Tools and Data,* and *Applications.*

The Research Brief sections present concise summaries of actual studies, including descriptions of the decisions and/or challenges they posed for the researchers. Assessment questions follow each brief to help you examine these typical research decisions and challenges.

The Tools and Data sections explain the "nuts and bolts" of research by illustrating a variety of investigative tools and data that are part of the research process. The accompanying assessment questions will help to develop your research skills.

The Application sections provide research activities for you to conduct on your own. These mini-projects will give you a real taste of what social research is all about.

The final chapter contains a wide range of interviews with prominent social researchers. Their comments offer insights into the human element of research—the motivations, challenges, experiences, and decisions that shape the researcher's role.

As you proceed through this book, you will discover the importance of three key issues in numerous research decisions: (1) the influence of bias, (2) the effects of research on human subjects, and (3) the contrast between scientific orientation and common sense. These issues are important elements of the social research process and are concerns with which the researcher must grapple. Let us take a moment to explain their effects on the research process.

Bias

People often misinterpret new information because of preconceived notions. For example, German shepherds are widely assumed to be vicious because they are frequently used as attack dogs. Therefore, many people are unwilling to approach a German shepherd, even though it may be perfectly tame and friendly. Even some individuals who own German shepherds display this bias toward other German shepherds.

Your attitudes toward life influence the way in which you perceive things. For instance, if I ask you whether a glass is half full or half empty, your answer may depend on whether you are optimistic or pessimistic. Thus, it cannot be assumed that you will reach the same conclusion about an observation as others. Researchers constantly face this same dilemma, since they too have accumulated many preconceived notions about the social world. How can they be trusted to question, observe, and analyze human behavior and interactions objectively and accurately?

Bias not only influences our visual observations; it affects oral communication as well. The selective hearing process is demonstrated in Gorgon Allport and Leo Postman's classic experimental research (1947) on rumor transmission, which traced the gradual changes in the content of rumors over time. This study showed that rumors typically became shorter, limited to fewer details, and transformed to be consistent with the belief system of the participants. A rumor about an ambulance carrying explosives, for example, evolved into a rumor about an ambulance carrying medical supplies, which was more consistent with people's preconceived notions about an ambulance's proper function.

Take a moment to test your own biases. Look at the photograph below, taken from a brochure published by the Sociology Department at Pacific Lutheran University in Tacoma, Washington. Which of the two people in the photo is the graduate and which is the professor?

Did you guess that the professor was the man? Most people do. Actually, however, the photo is of Professor Kathleen O'Connor posing with a former student who had just been granted his B.S. degree. Nevertheless, there are valid preconceptions that might lead one to assume that Professor O'Connor is the student here. Statistically, there are more male than female professors, which inclines us to assign the professor's role to the man. Visually, the student is taller than the professor and appears more imposing—both visual cues of power—which also can be misleading.

As you can see, controlling or measuring bias is a vital aspect of the research process. Fortunately, many techniques have been developed to assist us in this challenge. To draw objective conclusions, we must first be fully aware of the role that bias plays in our inquiries, observations, and conclusions.

Human Subjects

Social research frequently involves the study of human subjects—what they think, believe, desire, and value and how they behave within the context of various social settings such as families, schools, markets, political arenas, businesses, religious organizations, the military, rural areas, and cities. There are two principal ways to study human subjects: question them or watch them. Either way, there is a risk of disparity between perception and reality.

Suppose, for example, that you set out to study equality in the workplace, focusing on why there are more men than women in upper management positions. Mary Frank Fox and Sharlene Hess-Biber (1984) reported that women comprise only one percent of vice presidents, and that only six percent of middle managers are women. Furthermore, women with managerial titles are most commonly found in lower-level positions, such as supervisors, department heads, and office managers.

The design for your supposed study includes a survey questionnaire for male corporate executives to determine reasons for the imbalance reported by Fox and Hess-Biber. Surprisingly, the results of your research show that top executives believe in equal opportunity for women. If this observation is correct, why then do so few women hold top managerial positions?

There are many possible explanations for this contradiction. Since your study focused exclusively on the attitudes of executives in a position to hire female managers, does this mean that sexism and negative views of female managerial capabilities on the part of these executives have to be ruled out?

It is difficult to answer this question without examining the details of your survey. For example, consider the following questions: (1) Could the executives have been trying to make a favorable impression on you by saying what they thought you wanted to hear? If, for example, you are a female, would they want to appear supportive of you as a woman in a career position? (2) Did your study include ways to detect discrepancies between the executives' professed attitudes and their actual behavior, such as checking their records on promoting females to top managerial positions?

Observing human behavior entails similar problems. Can researchers observe actual behavior without changing it in the process? Will study subjects become inhibited or self-protective in the presence of an observer? Will people put on an act to present themselves in a positive light or try to portray themselves as they want to be portrayed?

Another potential problem in studying human subjects is the issue of ethics. Some research designs may expose human subjects to harmful consequences.

Researchers must be sensitive to all the risks—psychological, physical, social, political, or economic—that might be incurred by their subjects. Studies must be carefully designed to protect participants from such risks. In some cases it may be decided that the information gained from the research might not be worth the risk to the study participants.

A classic example of this ethical dilemma is found in the Milgram obedience experiment (Kelman 1968). Although the actual purpose of the research was to study obedience to authority, the research subjects were led to believe that they were participating in an experiment on the effect of punishment on learning. Assigned the role of teachers in a test situation, the subjects were instructed to administer electric shocks to their pupils every time they failed to give correct answers. The subjects' degree of compliance was surprisingly high. Despite vehement pleas for mercy from the pupils, most of the subjects administered intense levels of pain. They did not know at the time that the electric shocks were fake and the pupils, who were actually hired actors, were accomplices of the experimenters in misleading the subjects. The experiment, however, had an unexpected after-effect. Though the pupils suffered no real harm and the research subjects were subsequently informed of the deception, many of the more obedient subjects suffered severe guilt and experienced psychological problems ranging from stress to convulsions.

Milgram's work has been extensively criticized on the grounds that it took advantage of naive research subjects. Defendants of the study claim, however, that it is an invaluable contribution to the study of human choice. Only through understanding the nature of obedience under adverse circumstances, they argue, can society create social conditions which encourage people to resist authority and exercise freedom of choice.

Do you believe that Milgram was justified in causing psychological harm to his subjects in order to teach society a valuable lesson? If you had conducted this research project, could you have found a way to better protect the subjects? Ethical decisions regarding the treatment of human subjects play a vital role in the research process. Researchers are constantly challenged to weigh the risks of research against the benefits of the knowledge gained.

Common Sense

How different is the scientific approach to research from the common sense approach we all use to understand the world? What are the dangers of using common sense as part of the research process? Conversely, are there risks involved in keeping common sense out of the process?

The scientific approach to research provides well-defined rules for investigating the world, but common sense also plays a valuable role. The key challenge here for researchers is to maintain a scientific methodology without losing sight of common sense.

One application of the scientific approach to research involves the "logic of disconfirmation," which encourages the researcher to seek evidence that disproves his or her hypotheses. In the case of statistically-oriented research, each hypothesis which guides the investigation is initially stated negatively as a *null hypothesis*. Suppose, for example, that a researcher expects income levels to differ according to educational background and predicts that the average salary for college graduates will be higher than that for high school graduates. The null hypothesis, designed to contradict this assumption, is worded as follows: "There is no difference between the average salary earned by high school graduates and college graduates." The onus falls on the researcher to find sufficiently compelling data to warrant a rejection of the null hypothesis.

Non-statistical research approaches, such as the participant observation design whereby researchers become personally involved in the social settings under study, applies a similar strategy. Participant observers actively seek a full range of data by varying times, places, and participants. Rather than trying to prove that their set of beliefs is correct, they strive to identify the patterns of attitudes, beliefs, behavior, etc., that are woven into the social fabric. Their interpretations are continuously revised throughout the study period, as they uncover certain exceptions and integrate them into subsequent interpretations. Researchers can only reach their final conclusions when they are satisfied that they have found all anomalies to the general patterns.

The scientific approach applied to both statistical and non-statistical research designs is not the usual way of making sense of the world. Normally, people make assertions and gather evidence to prove themselves right. The following hypothetical example illustrates this distinction:

A woman travels to a distant city to visit a former college roommate. Before she leaves, several people warn her that the people in this city are generally rude and unfriendly. Because her friend has to work the first day of her visit, the woman decides to spend the day exploring the city on foot. During her walk, she notices that no passers-by look at her or say hello. She even finds it difficult to strike up a conversation with the waitress or the customers sitting next to her at a deli where she stops for lunch. By early afternoon she has become tense and anxious. She feels as if she is surrounded by a hostile environment, so she cuts short her walking tour and returns early to her friend's apartment. When her friend comes home from work, the visitor reports her observations about the people she encountered that day, wondering how her friend can live amidst such hostility. To her surprise, the friend adamantly disagrees with her, describing all the wonderful friends she has made in this city and all her incredibly warm, helpful co-workers. In fact, she claims, she chose to relocate to this city primarily because its job recruiters had been so friendly when they had visited her campus the previous year.

How could the interpretations of these two friends differ so radically? Which one is correct?

From the standpoint of common sense, both are correct. Each woman formed opinions based on her own personal experience and what she wanted to believe. As is typically the case, their observations matched what they expected to find in order to prove themselves right. From a scientific standpoint, a more systematic method of data collection and clarification of research variables would have to be established before any conclusions could be reached. The logic of disconfirmation would also have to be employed.

By the same token, however, the judgments of these two friends helped to shape the direction of their inquiry. The visitor's perception of hostility was based on that of a complete stranger in an unknown city, while her friend's perception of friendliness was based on pre-established affiliations in a workplace environment. The common sense mode of observation is a valid tool in the development of conceptualization, hypothesis development, and data collection strategies. When researchers dismiss common sense as non-scientific, they run the risk of not asking appropriate and important questions and omitting critical variables, e.g., race, gender, and ethnicity, thereby misinterpreting their data (Crawley and Ecker 1990).

Managing the balance between common sense and the "logic of discon-firmation" is like walking a tightrope. Biases must not be allowed to control the research process; yet, on the other hand, important insights that may be derived from common sense observations should not be ignored.

Are you ready to walk the tightrope between scientific methods and common sense? Can you recognize your own biases and how they affect your percep-tions? Are you willing to meet the challenges inherent in studies involving human subjects? Working through the chapters in this book will help you to answer these questions as you experience firsthand the decisions, choices, and constraints that are part of the research process.

Chapter 2

From Mental Health to Gender Equity: Selecting Research Topics

✔ *Research Brief:*

Mental Illness and the Homeless

✔ *Tools and Data:*

Selecting a Topic in Order to Obtain
Federal Funding for Research

✔ *Application:*

How Specific Can You Get?

Chapter 2

Research Brief:

Mental Illness and the Homeless

A subject of continuing interest to researchers, as well as to governmental agencies and the general public, is the mental health of the homeless. There have been two research groups who selected this topic for different reasons: one headed by David Snow, which conducted basic research, and another under the direction of co-author Jane Reisman. The latter was commissioned by a city government to conduct contract research on this issue.

David Snow and three colleagues (Snow, et al., 1986) began their study of homelessness during the middle 1980s. Like many others in academia and government, they were interested in both the number of homeless and the type of people who comprise this group. Most of the previous research on this subject was psychiatrically-oriented, specifically to determine the existence of a high level of mental illness among the homeless. Snow and his colleagues, however, discovered that many of the findings from this research did not concur with those from other studies that were not psychiatrically-based. For example, a large-scale study conducted in Ohio reported a relatively low incidence of serious psychiatric symptoms among the homeless (Roth, et al., 1985).

Snow's group further observed that the media appeared to play up findings purporting high levels of mental illness, while down-playing less sensational characterizations of the homeless as victims of such social and economic factors as unemployment, insufficient income, and a scarcity of affordable housing. The researchers believed that the manner in which the homeless are portrayed has important implications for society. Understanding the underlying reasons for homelessness could be critical to the development of appropriate social policies to deal with the problem.

Thus, a research topic was born: the actual proportion of homeless living in or passing through a city (in this case, Austin, Texas) who could be designated as mentally ill. The study focused on "unattached, adult, homeless street people living in urban areas whose lifestyle is characterized by the absence of permanent housing, supportive familial bonds, and consensually defined roles of social utility and moral worth."

Snow and his colleagues employed two research strategies: extensive ethnographic fieldwork, which involved interacting with and observing 164 homeless individuals on the streets for 12 months, and a 15-month tracking of a random sample of 767 homeless through their contacts with social services institutions.

The second study, headed by Jane Reisman in collaboration with faculty and graduate students from the Division of Social Sciences at Pacific Lutheran University, evolved in a very different fashion from Snow's study. In this case, the city council of Tacoma, Washington, wanted more information about its homeless population in order to deal with it more effectively. It commissioned Pacific Lutheran University to do a study covering a four-month period between October, 1986, and January, 1987.

The objective of the study was "to establish the character and magnitude of the challenges that local government agencies, private organizations, and the local community face in dealing with mentally disordered street people" (Reisman, et al., 1987, pp. 4-5). The following information was sought:

1. The approximate number of mentally disturbed street people in the downtown area of Tacoma, as well as those who might episodically fit that category;

2. The general circumstances of the study group, including information related to shelter, food, finances, residency, health, and personal safety;

3. The manner in which such people interact with government agencies, private agencies, businesses, and the citizens of Tacoma;

4. The manner in which agencies exercise control over these people when control/treatment is deemed necessary (for example, involuntary treatment, the response of law enforcement, arrests, trials, imprisonment, etc.); and

5. The cost to the public sector, private sector, and the community of contacting and processing mentally disturbed street people.

The researchers worked closely with an advisory committee appointed by the city, which consisted of representatives from a number of sectors, including the downtown business community, shelter providers, mental health services, and a state psychiatric hospital. The purpose of this committee was to provide input to determine the practicality and appropriateness of various research approaches.

The research involved observing street people, interviewing 72 of the mentally disordered from a representative sample, and interviewing "key informants" from shelters, government agencies, downtown businesses, mental health facilities, and protective services. The mentally disordered of the homeless were defined as such by shelter staff and the street people themselves. (Objective criteria, including the incidence of alcohol and drug addiction, and the history of psychiatric treatment, institutionalization, or medication for psychiatric problems, were used to validate these designations.) Escorts were recruited from the homeless population in order to introduce the researchers to potential respondents and help gain acceptance and approval for their participation in the study.

The data generated from this research formed the basis for city policy decisions regarding the homeless and were also successfully used by the staff of mental health facilities, government agencies, and homeless shelters in their efforts to obtain financial support from external sources.

ASSESSMENT QUESTIONS
for *Research Brief*, Chapter 2

Name_____Date_____

Answer the following questions based on the research brief just presented:

1. Which of the following appears to be a consideration in Snow, et al.'s selection of a research topic?

    a. government agency funding
    b. the psychiatric orientation of most research on the topic
    c. sympathy for the homeless population
    d. the need for research publications to obtain tenure at their universities.

2. Which of the following appears to be a consideration in Reisman, et al.'s selection of a research topic?

    a. government agency funding
    b. the psychiatric orientation of most research on the topic
    c. sympathy for the homeless population
    d. the need for research publications to obtain tenure at their university

3. What is a major difference between the two studies in terms of how the topics were selected?

4. Discuss one way in which dealing with human subjects (i.e., the homeless) might have been a consideration in *refining* the topic selection for each study. In doing so, address the importance of ethics in terms of potential risks to the homeless population.

    a. Snow Study

    b. Reisman Study

Chapter 2

Tools and Data:
Selecting a Topic in Order to Obtain Federal Funding for Research

Jeanne Kohl, one of this book's co-authors, has been involved in teaching and research on educational equity, gender bias, and methods of promoting gender equity in the schools. One of her areas of interest is the participation of women in school athletics. She wanted to conduct independent research outside the university on this topic and needed a source of funding to support her work.

Kohl learned of an "RFP" (Request for Proposal) issued by the Women's Educational Equity Act Program of the U.S. Department of Education to solicit proposals for the funding of projects concerning women's educational equity. She then obtained the application materials and submitted a funding proposal. Researchers seldom enjoy preparing federal grant proposals since they usually require a great deal of detail and organization, and this proposal was no exception. Fortunately, it was selected for funding, and Kohl was awarded a $40,000 grant.

An important part of a grant proposal is the *abstract*, which provides a brief summary of the research questions and objectives and, in most cases, the overall intent of the study. Kohl's abstract stated:

Although the rate of female student participation in secondary school sports *increased* dramatically with the passage of Title IX, it has had periods of decline and rise since its high point in 1977-78. However, the proportion of women as high school coaches, trainers, officials, and sports administrators has steadily and dramatically *declined* during this time. Also, there is a notable under-representation of racial and ethnic minority women as athletes and coaches.

This proposed project focuses on the promotion of educational equity for girls and women through researching state laws concerning school athletics and gender discrimination and equity, student participation rates, participation rates of women in coaching and sports administration, and coaching certification. The project will develop a guide, *Girls and Women in School Sports: A Guide to Participation and*

Coaching Certification, which will be an invaluable resource for policymakers, state legislators, school district personnel, state athletic associations, women in sports organizations, parents, and students.

In order to ensure the continuation as well as increase in participation of girls and women in sports, it is important to increase the percentage of women in coaching, officiating, and administrating of school sports teams and programs. Related to this is the urgent need to develop and standardize certification requirements for coaches, which will assist to encourage women and expand opportunities for them to seek and achieve these positions. Working to increase the percentage of women in these positions will serve to promote educational equity for women and girls.

The project will work toward achieving four goals in its striving to meet its objectives, including that of preparing the Guide. These goals involve researching: 1) athletic participation rates of secondary school girls; 2) coaching and administrative participation of women; 3) recruitment and certification requirements of coaching, officiating, and administrative positions; and 4) plans for model standardized coaching recruitment and certification requirements.

ASSESSMENT QUESTIONS
for *Tools and Data,* Chapter 2

*Name*_____*Date*_____

Read the following excerpts taken from the RFP issued by the Women's Educational Equity Act Program to prospective applicants. Then answer the questions that follow which pertain to Kohl's funding proposal.

Purpose of Program: To promote educational equity for women and girls, particularly those who suffer multiple discrimination, bias, or stereotyping, and to provide assistance to agencies and institutions to meet the requirements of Title IX of the Education Amendments of 1972 [federal law prohibiting sex discrimination in educational institutions].

Estimated Range of Awards: Challenge Grants: $30,000-$40,000; General Grants: $50,000-$200,000.

Estimated Number of Awards: Challenge Grants: 15; General Grants: 15.

Priority: In establishing priorities for funding each year . . . the Secretary may select one or more of the following:

(a) Projects to develop and test model programs and materials that could be used by local educational agencies and other entities in meeting the requirements of Title IX.

(b) Projects to develop new educational programs, training programs, counseling programs, or other programs designed to increase the interest and participation of women in instructional courses in mathematics, science, and computer science.

(c) Projects to develop new educational programs, training programs, counseling programs, or other programs, or to expand existing model programs designed to accomplish the following:

(1) Reduce the rate at which women drop out of formal education.

(2) Encourage women dropouts to resume their education.

(d) Projects to develop or expand guidance and counseling programs designed to increase the knowledge and awareness of women regarding opportunities in careers in which women have not significantly participated.

(e) Projects to develop new educational programs or expand existing model educational programs designed to enhance opportunities for educational achievement by economically disadvantaged women.

(f) Projects to develop new educational programs or expand existing model educational programs designed to enhance opportunities for educational achievement by women who suffer multiple discrimination on the basis of sex and race, ethnic origin, age, or disability.

Who is eligible for an award? The following are eligible to receive awards under the Women's Educational Equity Act Program:

(a) Public agencies, institutions, and organizations.

(b) Nonprofit private agencies, institutions, and organizations, including student and community groups.

(c) Individuals.

Answer the following questions:

1. Identify one way in which Kohl's proposed project (as described in the Abstract) meets the requirements listed under *Purpose of Program.*

2. For which type of grant do you believe Kohl would have applied?

___ Challenge Grant   ___ General Grant

Why?

3. Which one of the *priorities* listed in the RFP do you believe was the most relevant to Kohl's proposed project?

___ a   ___ b   ___ c   ___ d   ___ e   ___ f

Why?

4. Which category of *eligibility* do you think Kohl used in applying for this grant?

    ____   (a) Public agencies, institutions, and organizations.

    ____   (b) Nonprofit private agencies, institutions, and organizations, including student and community groups.

    ____   (c) Individuals.

5. What product did Kohl propose to develop as part of her project?

6. In contrast to this more "applied" type of research study, what might be a topic for a "basic research" study about girls and women in school sports?

Chapter 2

Application:
How Specific Can You Get?

Name_____Date_____

1. State a *specific* topic or problem for a research study on the following broad issues. State the topic or problem in the form of a research question. Be sure to phrase your questions so that they specify a relationship between two or more variables.

Example:

Issue

Research Question

a. poverty and children

Do children living in impoverished families miss school more frequently than do children living in middle- and upper-class families?

Issue

Research Question

b. gender and alcohol

c. political party affiliation and social class

d. work problems and marital status

Issue   *Research Question*

   e. college attendance
      and race/ethnicity

   f. drug addiction, parents,
      and educational attainment

   g. senior citizens and sexuality

2. Formulate a research question that might be asked by each of the entities listed below about the causes or consequences of child sex abuse. Consider some of the following areas that may apply to each question: children, sexual abuse, schools, family income, and a state agency to provide assistance to children and their families.

Entity   *Research Question*

   a. a school district

   b. a city government

   c. the U.S. Department
      of Education

   d. a university professor
      conducting independent
      research

   e. a student enrolled in a
      research methods course

3. Suppose you are interested in doing research on the general topic of dating violence and social class. However, you are not sure how to make this broad topic more specific. List three things below that you might do to narrow your topic so that it will be a viable subject for research.

   a.

   b.

   c.

Chapter 3

Which Approach to Use: Choices and Constraints

✓ **Research Brief:**

Do Women on Welfare Keep Having Babies
in Order to Continue Collecting Welfare?

✓ **Tools and Data:**

Communication: The Key to a Good Relationship

✓ **Application:**

Program Evaluation Design

Chapter 3

Research Brief:

Do Women on Welfare Keep Having Babies in Order to Continue Collecting Welfare?

Few issues provoke as much controversy as that of welfare. At one end of the spectrum we may hear that people on welfare are lazy, that they do not want to work, or that women keep getting pregnant so they can stay on welfare. At the other end we may hear that welfare recipients have been oppressed by a capitalistic system and are on welfare through no fault of their own.

Mark R. Rank (1989) conducted research on the incidence and determinants of fertility among women on welfare in the state of Wisconsin. He was particularly interested in the likelihood of childbearing among women on welfare and whether their fertility rate was higher or lower than that of women in the general population.

Rank found that previous research on these issues tended to focus on illegitimacy rates rather than fertility rates. This research consisted primarily of cross-sectional studies in which welfare mothers were expected to rely on recall as to the time of their pregnancies. The longitudinal studies did not gather information on exactly when these women were in or out of the welfare system. Also, most studies used either very small or non-random samples which did not have an adequate basis for making reliable fertility estimates. Furthermore, they lacked the use of appropriate comparison groups to judge whether the fertility rates of women on welfare were high or low.

In contrast to the design of these studies, Rank's research design used a large random sample, which he followed longitudinally over a three-year period. He compared the fertility and welfare time rates of his sample with those of a national comparison group of women aged 18–44. In addition, he conducted in-depth qualitative interviews with a matched sample of welfare recipients to gain insight into the significance of his quantitative longitudinal data. Thus, Rank utilized two sources of data—one quantitative, the other qualitative—which were different yet complementary, since both were drawn in a like manner from similar populations.

How did Rank select his samples? The quantitative sample was obtained by randomly drawing two percent of welfare "case heads" (eligible recipients) or applicants who had been receiving one or more of three types of welfare assistance—AFDC (Aid to Families with Dependent Children), Food Stamps, and Medicaid—in Wisconsin as of September, 1980. Families were defined as the case head or applicant along with others residing in her household. This sample amounted to 2,796 households receiving public assistance—either as new cases or over varying lengths of time. The cases were followed for three years with reviews at six-month intervals. Case records, rather than data gathered from individuals, were used for analysis.

The qualitative sample was drawn from the case records of a representative county to provide a stratified random sample that would reflect the diversity of the state's population. Face-to-face interviews were conducted with 50 families (76 percent of the cases contacted). Each was paid $15. The interviews were open-ended, covering topics such as family dynamics, employment and welfare. In particular, women were asked about their attitudes toward childbearing, especially while on welfare.

In order to ensure accurate measurement of fertility rates, Rank used women in the same age bracket (18-44) in his two samples and comparison group. Also, he combined married and unmarried women in his calculations, which is standard practice in calculating national fertility rates. Women who went off welfare and later came back on were used only once in his sample, and only those who had been on welfare for at least nine months were included. This was particularly important in the case of women who entered the welfare system due to an impending birth. His primary focus was on the rate of welfare dependence leading to birth, as opposed to birth leading to welfare dependence.

In response to his question about the likelihood of childbearing, Rank found that the fertility rate for women on welfare was 45.8 (the number of births per 1,000 women aged 18-44). The response to his second question regarding comparison to other groups showed fertility rates of 75.3 in Wisconsin and 71.1 nationwide. Comparatively, then, the fertility rates of women on welfare were significantly lower than those of the general female population in the state and the nation.

Women on welfare, however, tended to differ in demographic variables, such as race, marital status, education, and age, from women in the general population. Therefore, Rank subsequently compared the fertility rate of his samples with one of similar demographic makeup in the general population. He again found that the fertility rates for these women on welfare, ranging from 25.3 to 47.8 percent, were considerably lower than national population figures and 29.2 to 54.4 percent lower than Wisconsin's.

Using qualitative data from interviews, Rank explored the reasons behind the lower fertility rates among the sample women receiving welfare. He found that the longer they were on welfare, the less likely they were to give birth. The majority of the 50 women interviewed had borne one or two children, and only two were pregnant at the time of their interviews. None of the 48 non-pregnant women wanted children in the near future. They reported that their situations would likely worsen if they became pregnant. In addition, virtually all said that they wanted to get off welfare, which would be less likely if they were pregnant. Analysis of the interview data revealed that pregnancies were more likely to be accidental than planned.

Thus, Rank's analysis did not support assumptions often made by social and policy analysts that women on welfare have higher fertility rates. The design he selected for his research and analysis provided new insights into this controversial and inadequately addressed topic.

ASSESSMENT QUESTIONS
for *Research Brief,* Chapter 3

*Name*_____*Date*_____

Mark Rank designed his study on the fertility rates of women on welfare to address what he believed to be inadequacies in prior research conducted on the topic. Answer the following questions pertaining to Rank's research design.

1. Which of the following was *not* discussed by Rank as a shortcoming of prior research regarding fertility rates of women on welfare?

   a. reliability checks
   b. sample selections
   c. analyses limited to survey data without also using case records
   d. a lack of comparison group(s)

2. Describe two approaches used by Rank to ensure an accurate determination of fertility rates.

   a.

   b.

3. What was the rationale for including a comparison group in Rank's study?

4. What did Rank do to eliminate bias and ensure the accuracy of his finding of a lower fertility rate for women on welfare than for women in the general population?

5. Why did Rank use both qualitative and quantitative data analyses?

6. Name two findings from Rank's qualitative analysis that would account for what he found in his quantitative analysis.

   a.

   b.

Chapter 3

Tools and Data:
Communication: The Key to a Good Relationship

Communication in relationships has been a topic frequently studied by social researchers. Many different approaches have been taken to gain a more thorough understanding of its importance, as well as of relationships in general. Two such approaches and the research tools used in each case will be discussed in this section.

Philip Blumstein's and Pepper Schwartz's book, *American Couples: Money, Work, and Sex,* published in 1983, recounted their large-scale, in-depth research on couples. This study, a follow-up to their earlier research on the communication of affection, reflected their growing interest in the entire spectrum of relationships between men and women.

The focus of Pamela Fishman's research (first published in the journal *Social Problems* in April, 1978) was more narrow in scope. She examined how the power relationship between men and women is communicated in conversation. While Blumstein and Schwartz surveyed thousands of couples, Fishman's sample consisted of only three couples.

Blumstein and Schwartz's research design had several objectives: (1) a large and diverse sample of respondents varying in income level, age, education, geographical residence, political values, religion, lifestyles, etc.; (2) data that would include statistical analysis obtained through the use of questionnaires, face-to-face interviews, and tape recordings of imaginary problem-solving scenarios; and (3) the ability to make predictions regarding the stability of relationships based on the results of questionnaires given to a large number of participating couples.

In contrast, Fishman designed her study around the taped conversations of three couples recorded in the privacy of their homes without the presence of a researcher. No questionnaires were completed, no interviews were conducted, and the couples retained the right to censor the taped material. The participants were all white, professionally-oriented, between 25 and 35 years of age, and sympathetic to the women's movement.

Fishman's research design was geared toward the use of normal conversations to conduct "an analysis of the interactional production of a particular reality through people's talk" (p. 398). She was particularly interested in learning how males and females differ in the "work of interaction." Analyses of her subjects' taped conversations affirmed the dominance of men in verbal interaction and the effort of women to sustain conversation through supportive responses.

Blumstein and Schwartz used a 38-page questionnaire to survey the individual partners of thousands of couples, including heterosexuals and gays, marrieds and unmarrieds. They obtained 12,000 usable questionnaires. They also interviewed 300 couples, individually and together, and privately tape-recorded many couples who participated in contrived scenarios. A large number of participants received follow-up questionnaires 18 months later. These methods produced a wealth of data.

Fishman, on the other hand, obtained data from 52 hours of conversations, recorded during periods ranging from four to 14 days among the three couples. Fishman selected three transcripts from five hours of conversations for her final data set.

In general then, Blumstein's and Schwartz's main research "tools" were their questionnaires and multiple interviews; Fishman's was her tape recorder. Below are examples of questions from the first study's questionnaire.

Relationship Questions

1. How satisfied are you with these parts of your relationship? (1 = extremely satisfied, 9 = not at all satisfied)

   c. The way we communicate.   1 2 3 4 5 6 7 8 9

4. Who is more likely to do each of the following things in your relationship, you or your partner? (1 = I do this much more, 5 = we do this equally, 9 = he/she does this much more)

   b. Try to see the other's point of view when we are having an argument.

      1 2 3 4 5 6 7 8 9

   d. Begin to talk about what is troubling our relationship when there is tension between us.   1 2 3 4 5 6 7 8 9

Blumstein's and Schwartz's vast findings were published in a 656-page book. Fishman's findings were reported in a 9-page journal article.

ASSESSMENT QUESTIONS
for *Tools and Data,* Chapter 3

Name_____Date_____

Consider the study of Blumstein and Schwartz with that of Fishman and complete the following:

1. Which study used a better basis for generalizing its findings based on the sampling method?

   ____ Blumstein and Schwartz

   ____ Fishman

2. Which study can better be applied to determining what was "normal" in couples' relationships?

   ____ Blumstein and Schwartz

   ____ Fishman

3. Identify the "tools" used in each study to collect data.

   a. Blumstein and Schwartz

      1.

      2.

      3.

   b. Fishman

      1.

4. Identify two potential problems with each study's approach (e.g., size of sample) and how these could affect the findings.

    a. Blumstein and Schwartz

        1.

        2.

    b. Fishman

        1.

        2.

5. Identify what you consider to be a major strength of each study's approach.

    a. Blumstein and Schwartz

    b. Fishman

Chapter 3

Application:
Program Evaluation Design

Name_____Date_____

Imagine that you have been asked to evaluate the effectiveness of an experimental juvenile restitution program in an impoverished Midwestern city. The purpose of the program is to reduce juvenile delinquency by sentencing youthful criminals to perform community service and make restitution to victims rather than be incarcerated. Since the program is heavily subsidized by the federal government, a U.S. Congressional Committee is very interested in the design and methods involved in this evaluation research and has submitted a list of questions for you. Provide answers to these questions in the space below.

1. What type of data will you be collecting?

    Why do you believe this type is important?

2. What time frame will you use?

    What is your rationale for taking this amount of time?

3. What will be your unit of analysis?

   Why?

4. How will you obtain your data?

   Why did you select this method over others?

5. Are any "human subjects" involved in your study?

   If so, who are they?

6. What potential risks might they incur?

7. How will you protect them from potential harm?

8. What political pressures do you expect to occur in the course of your research?

   How will you keep these pressures from influencing the research process?

Chapter 4

What Are You Thinking About? Conceptualization and Measurement

✓ **Research Brief:**

The Three Faces of Racism

✓ **Tools and Data:**

Conceptualizing and Measuring Intimacy

✓ **Applications:**

1. Conceptualization
2. Measurement

Chapter 4

Research Brief:
The Three Faces of Racism

Imagine yourself as a sociology graduate student at the University of California, Berkeley, in the 1960s. You have recently completed a master's thesis on black leadership in San Francisco. Professor Robert Blauner, whose work you find very exciting, has asked you to conduct part of his federally funded research on manhood orientations among black men. Naturally, you jump at the opportunity. If all goes well, the project will provide you with a valuable dissertation topic, a chance to work closely with a highly respected professor, and, perhaps most importantly, a full-time salary.

We have just described the origins of David Wellman's research on white racism in the United States, published in 1977 as *Portraits of White Racism*. After accepting the position, Wellman organized a research team and began to conceptualize the nature of racism. Interestingly, the members of Wellman's team differed from the highly educated, technically trained assistants who typically comprise a research staff. Recruited based on their affiliation with the black community to be studied, they included a longshoreman, a community worker, a "hippie" musician, a civil rights worker, and only one middle-class graduate student. "What impressed us about this original staff was their ability to talk about sensitive issues, to draw people out, and to understand the feelings of a variety of sectors of the black community" (Wellman 1977, p. 51).

Early on, some members of Wellman's team advised him that his proposed research had the wrong focus, despite its approval by a major federal funding source. Manhood, according to these assistants, was not a major topic of conversation in the black community. Early interview experiences drove this point home.

> Manhood issues in the black community were not nearly so salient as we had anticipated. Respondents were willing to talk about these issues but they sometimes

had to be prodded. The topic did not arise spontaneously as we had expected it would. People seemed more concerned with racism, power, and privilege. Some of our staff members had argued that this would be the case, and the situation seemed to validate their claims. As people who knew racial oppression from firsthand experience, they had been insisting that we look more closely at the realities of race rather than manhood. It became imperative that we revise and clarify our theoretical position. (Wellman, 1977, p. 56)

Refocusing the study on racism created new conceptual problems. Six months of intensive literature review revealed that sociologists, from the founders to the modern theorists, tended to view racism as an attitude problem stemming from prejudice. Racism and prejudice had become interchangeable terms. Two dimensions of prejudice were commonly discussed: hostility and faulty generalizations. Simpson and Yingers's definition of racial prejudice typified such conceptualization: "We shall define prejudice as an emotional, rigid attitude . . . toward a group of people. [It] involves not only prejudgment but . . . misjudgment as well. It is categorical thinking that systematically misinterprets the facts" (Wellman, 1977, pp. 4-5).

Conceptualizing racism in solely attitudinal terms suggests that education and enlightenment would solve the problem. If only people could be open-minded and properly informed, racism would cease to exist. Wellman could not accept this view. He felt that it portrayed racism in a vacuum, devoid of any social context or institutional involvement. The characterization of racism as faulty thinking by a few misguided people, an exception to the rule, failed to adequately explain its persistence and pervasiveness. Wellman's own interviews revealed that even liberal-minded individuals suffered from some form of racism.

Through intensive examination of interview data and by being receptive to new theoretical directions, Wellman reconceptualized the notion of racism for his research: he reclassified racism as a basic building block in society. Since the presence of racism affords exclusive privileges to white Americans, any real changes in race relations would mean a substantial loss of white privilege and stature. While people are willing to express sentiments in favor of equality, they prove less willing to accept a decline in their social position or economic standing. Given this perspective, it seemed unlikely that racism could be understood through questionnaire responses about prejudice, nor could it be corrected simply through education. Wellman described his alternative perception of racism as follows:

. . . Racism has various faces; it manifests itself to the world in different guises. Sometimes it appears as 'personal prejudice' which, it is argued here, is really a disguised way to defend privilege. Other times racism is manifested ideologically. Cultural and biological reasons are used as rationalizations and justifications for the superior position of whites. Racism is also expressed *institutionally* in the form of systematic practices that deny and exclude blacks from access to social resources. Recognizing that racism has at least three faces, or meanings, some social scientists argue that the three need to be clearly distinguished and separately analyzed . . . . However, the everyday workings of racism are not so neatly divided. People living in a racially stratified society maintain racism in each of its guises. Sometimes we can distinguish between them; usually we cannot. The ways in which racism is manifested are so intertwined, so much a part of each other, that they are often inseparable. Each is generated by and fundamentally interrelated to the structural issue of privilege. Thus, to see how white people 'do' racism in America we cannot compartmentalize their thoughts and actions; to see the full picture, the three distinct concepts need to be combined [emphasis added]. (1977, pp. 39-40)

Conceptualization and reconceptualization were critical aspects of Wellman's research. By changing the focus of his study from the problems associated with manhood to the role of racism in society, he was able to develop new ways to understand and address the tenacity of racist practices.

ASSESSMENT QUESTIONS
for *Research Brief,* Chapter 4

Name_____Date_____

Answer the following questions in relation to the study just presented:

1. Consider the role of bias in conceptualizing issues in race relations. Discuss the implications of bias in Wellman's shift of his research focus from manhood among black men to the concept of white privilege.

2. When is (are) the most opportune time(s) to consider conceptualization in the research process? How did Wellman's ongoing concern with conceptualization affect his study?

3. Imagine that you have to defend this research project to a review committee concerned about the protection of human subjects. List two risks the study might pose to your subjects. How can you protect them from negative consequences?

    (1) Risk:

       Protection:

    (2) Risk:

       Protection:

4. Which of the following outcomes can occur when the conceptualization of racism is limited to attitudinal dimensions?

    a. Racism is portrayed as an exception, not a rule.
    b. The position of racism in the social structure is ignored.
    c. Racism is reduced to misunderstandings and mistakes.
    d. The potential benefits of racism to white Americans are disguised.
    e. None of the above.
    f. All of the above.

5. Place an *N* next to the nominal definition (a definition which identifies the elements of the concept in question) of racism and an *O* next to the operational definition (a definition which identifies specific observable indicators that measure the concept in question).

    ____ Observational data which document the advantageous position of white Americans, e.g., statements supporting a belief in the biological superiority of white people, unfavorable treatment of black applicants applying for credit, favoritism toward white job applicants, and derogatory language used in reference to black people.

    ____ A building block of society which affords exclusive privilege to white Americans.

Chapter **4**

Tools and Data:
Conceptualizing and Measuring Intimacy

Lillian B. Rubin's book, *Intimate Strangers: Men and Women Together,* published in 1983, questions the magic of "getting married and living happily ever after." As a social scientist and psychotherapist, Rubin collected a wealth of data on the experiences of couples from all walks of life. Intimacy, she argues, is a "persistent strain" on the committed relationships between men and women.

The following excerpt from Rubin's book analyzes the concept of intimacy. As you read it, consider how she refines the concept of intimacy and its implications for measurement decisions.

INTIMACY. WE HUNGER FOR IT, but we also fear it. We come close to a loved one, then we back off. A teacher I had once described this as the "go away a little closer" message. I call it the approach-avoidance dance.

The conventional wisdom says that women want intimacy, men resist it. And I have plenty of material that would seem to support that view. Whether in my research interview, in my clinical hours, or in the ordinary course of my life, I hear the same story told repeatedly. "He doesn't talk to me," says a woman. "I don't know what she wants me to talk about," says a man. "I want to know what he's feeling," she tells me. "I'm not feeling anything," he insists. "Who can feel nothing?" she cries. "I can," he shouts. As the heat rises, so does the wall between them. Defensive and angry, they retreat—stalemated by their inability to understand each other.

The expression of such conflicts would seem to validate the common understandings that suggest that women want and need intimacy more than men do—that the issue belongs to women alone; that if left to themselves, men would not suffer it. But things are not always what they seem . . .

Asked what intimacy is, most of us—men and women—struggle to say something sensible, something that we can connect with the real experience of our lives. "Intimacy is knowing there's someone who cares about the children as much as you do." "Intimacy is a history of shared experience." "It's sitting there having a cup of coffee together and watching the eleven o'clock news." "It's knowing you care about the same things." "It's knowing she'l always understand." "It's him sitting in the hospital for hours at a time when I was sick." "It's knowing he cares when I'm hurting." "It's standing by me when I was out of work." "It's seeing each other at our worst." "It's sitting across the breakfast table." "It's talking when you're in the bathroom." "It's knowing we'l begin and end each day together."

These seem the obvious things—the things we expect when we commit our lives to one another in a marriage, when we decide to have children together. And they're not to be dismissed as inconsequential. They make up the daily experience of our lives together, setting the tone for a relationship in important and powerful ways. It's sharing such commonplace, everyday events that determines the temper and the texture of life, that keeps us living together even when other aspects of the relationship seem less than perfect. Knowing someone is there, is constant, and can be counted on in just the ways these thoughts express provides the background of emotional security and stability we look for when we enter a marriage. Certainly a marriage and the people in it will be tested and judged quite differently in an unusual situation or in a crisis. But how often does life present us with circumstances and events that are so out of the range of ordinary experience?

These ways in which a relationship feels intimate on a daily basis are only part of what we mean by intimacy, however—the part that's most obvious, the part that doesn't awaken our fears. At a lecture where I spoke of these issues recently, one man commented also, "Intimacy is putting aside the masks we wear in the rest of our lives." A murmur of assent ran through the audience of a hundred or so. Intuitively, we say "yes." Yet this is the very issue that also complicates our intimate relationships.

On the one hand, it's reassuring to be able to put away the public persona—to believe we can be loved for who we really are, that we can show our shadow side without fear, that our vulnerabilities will not be counted against us. "The most important thing is to feel I'm accepted just the way I am," people will say.

But there's another side. For when we show ourselves thus without masks, we also become anxious and fearful. "Is it possible that someone could love the real me?" we're likely to ask. Not the most promising question for the further development of intimacy, since it suggests that, whatever else another might do or feel, it's we who have trouble loving ourselves. Unfortunately, such misgivings are not usually experienced consciously. We're aware only that our discomfort has risen, that we feel a need to get away. For the person who has seen the "real me" is also the one who reflects back to us an image that's usually not wholly to our liking. We get angry at that, first at ourselves for not living up to our own expectations, than at the other, who becomes for us the mirror of our self-doubts—a displacement of hostility that serves intimacy poorly.

There's yet another level—one that's further below the surface of consciousness, therefore, one that's much more difficult for us to grasp, let alone to talk about. I'm referring to the differences in the ways in which women and men deal with their inner emotional lives—differences that create barriers between us that can be high indeed.

Stop a woman in mid-sentence with the question, "What are you feeling right now?" and you might have to wait a bit while she reruns the mental tape to capture the moment just passed. But, more than likely, she'l be able to do it successfully. More than likely, she'll think for a while and come up with an answer.

The same is not true of a man. For him, a similar question usually will bring a sense of wonderment that one would even ask it, followed quickly by an uncomprehending and puzzled response. "What do you mean?" he'l ask. "I was just talking," he'll say. . . .

Repeatedly when therapy begins, I find myself having to go teach a man how to monitor his internal states—how to attend to his thoughts and feelings, how to bring them into consciousness. In the early stages of our work, it's a common experience to say to a man, "How does that feel?" and to see a blank look come over his face. Over and over, I find myself listening as a man speaks with calm reason about a situation which I know must be fraught with pain. "How do you feel about that?" I'l ask. "I've just been telling you," he's likely to reply. "No," I'l say, "you've told me what happened, not how you feel about it." Frustrated, he might well respond, "You sound just like my wife." (Rubin, 1983, pp. 65-70)

ASSESSMENT QUESTIONS
for *Tools and Data,* Chapter 4

*Name*_____*Date*_____

Consider Rubin's discussion of intimacy in completing the following exercises.

1. Develop a nominal and an operational definition for intimacy.

   Nominal:

   Operational:

2. Describe two alternative approaches to measuring intimacy based on the operational definition developed above. List two positive and two negative features of each measurement approach.

   a. Approach:

      Pros: (1)

             (2)

      Cons: (1)

             (2)

   b. Approach:

Pros: (1)

(2)

Cons: (1)

(2)

3. With which of the following potential conceptual errors is Rubin concerned in her discussion of intimacy?

   a. Gender differences might not be taken into account.
   b. The role of intimacy in society's ideological sphere might be overlooked.
   c. Intimacy may be confused with romantic love.
   d. The differences between ethnic cultures might not be considered.
   e. All of the above.

4. Match indicators of intimacy with each of its three dimensions as discussed by Rubin: caring, exposure of inner selves, and sharing inner emotional lives. Write the appropriate indicator's letter in the space provided next to each dimension. (Note: There are two indicators per dimension.)

Dimensions:

1. Caring   ___   ___

2. Exposure of inner selves   ___   ___

3. Sharing inner emotional lives   ___   ___

Indicators

   a. Acting insecure
   b. Admitting fears
   c. Expressing concern about someone else's health
   d. Spending time together on a regular basis
   e. Acting vain
   f. Revealing prejudices

Chapter 4

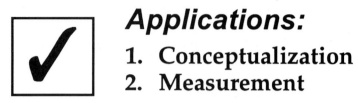

Applications:
1. Conceptualization
2. Measurement

Name_____Date_____

CONCEPTUALIZATION

Answer the questions below for one of the following terms: love, success, or talent.

1. Give a nominal definition of the concept.

2. Develop an operational definition of the concept.

3. Identify what you believe are the dimensions of the concept.

4. Develop an indicator for each dimension you identified

    Dimension: Indicator:

5. Identify any bias(es) you have regarding this concept that could influence your conceptualization and/or measurement of it.

6. Identify a potential problem concerning human subjects that could result from using this concept in research.

7. Discuss a potential error that could result from relying on common sense in defining this concept for research.

MEASUREMENT

Aggression has become a widely researched variable in both the social and natural sciences. One controversial topic of study related to aggression is sex and gender differences. While extensive research has indicated greater levels of aggressiveness in males than in females (Maccoby and Jacklin, 1974), research results have differed in regard to the size and level of variance and the interpretations of the data.

According to Lips (1988), several factors may be involved, such as the type of research method used, the age of subjects, the immediacy of the research, variations in gender socialization patterns, and changes in the researchers' perceptions. Conceptualization and measurement may be another major factor. How is aggression defined in the study? Is it measured by direct observation, experimentation, or responses to questionnaires or interviews? Could subject bias influence a researcher's perception of aggression and its comparative degrees between subjects? Condry and Ross (1985) found that college students were more likely to assume that a child was aggressive if they thought it was a boy. (The child in question was dressed in a manner that obscured its sex.) Also, many researchers have found that males and females may display different kinds of aggressiveness, either physical or verbal, which are affected or reinforced by rewards or punishments for aggressive acts. There is also controversy regarding the causes of these sexual differences, e.g., biological, psychological, social psychological, or cultural. Certainly, society transmits strong messages about aggression and gender, which can be more pronounced in some cultural groups than others.

Exercise:

Consider how you might go about conceptualizing aggression and measuring the possible differences (or similarities) in aggressiveness between males and females. Then, complete the following:

1. Ask five people for their definition of aggressiveness. Record their replies here.

    1.

    2.

    3.

    4.

    5.

2. After each of the five definitions, write an *N* or an *O* to indicate whether the definition seems to be nominal or operational.

3. Select one of the definitions and give dimensions for it along with an indicator for each dimension.

   Dimensions: Indicator:

4. Describe how you might go about measuring aggressiveness

   on the part of preschoolers:

   on the part of college students:

   on the part of senior citizens:

5. Give one example each of a potential risk in measurement associated with bias, working with human subjects, and common sense in a study of aggressiveness in dating situations.

   Bias:

   Human Subjects:

   Common Sense:

Chapter 5

'How Are You Feeling Today?' Operationalization and Instrumentation

✓ *Research Brief:*

Death and Dying in the Medical Environment

✓ *Tools and Data:*

The First Draft

✓ *Application:*

Guttman Scale

Chapter 5

Research Brief:
Death and Dying
in the Medical Environment

Death, in spite of its frequency and certainty, was not a common area of sociological concern until recently. David Sudnow's (1967) research was one of the initial studies in a recent wave of inquiry. Sudnow was interested in how death and dying were managed in medical settings. Using an ethnographic research design, he became a non-participant observer in two municipal hospitals: a large, charity hospital and a private, general one. He focused on the behavior of hospital staff members on the occasions of death and dying.

As a non-participant observer, Sudnow himself became the instrument of his research. Since he could not rely on carefully developed survey indexes and scales or organized content analysis procedures to obtain data objectively and systematically, he had to retrain his eyes and ears to collect data accurately and consistently, relying primarily on first-hand observations and casual conversations. His first few attempts to record actual conversations clandestinely were unsuccessful because of the hospitals' high levels of background noise. He held a few structured interviews, but these were mainly to study characteristics of these hospitals.

Sudnow's book about his research, *Passing On: The Social Organization of Dying* (1967), offers important insights into some of the challenges of instrumentation associated with non-participant observation techniques, including routine acceptance, flexibility, and the capacity to achieve objectivity.

How does an observer minimize his or her presence and become a "fly on the wall?" Sudnow set out to become routinely accepted by the hospital staff by standing around, attending routine rounds, witnessing procedures, sitting in public areas such as waiting rooms and cafeterias, and befriending individuals who would serve as informants. Initially the staff members were self-conscious and inhibited around him, but over several months they grew accustomed to his constant presence. Eventually he became a commonplace part of the hospital setting. In his view, ". . . I felt sufficiently disregarded to be relatively secure that what I was witnessing would have gone on were I not around" (1967, p. 7).

Nevertheless, a few incidents occurred during the course of the study in which the effect of Sudnow's presence became a factor. One such instance involved a group of interns fresh out of medical school, who could not seem to adjust to Sudnow's "invisible" presence. Instead, they were eager to demonstrate their medical knowledge and would occasionally even enlist Sudnow's aid in propping up a terminal patient or transferring the body of a deceased patient from a bed to a stretcher. Sudnow interpreted their behavior as a way for them to feel more comfortable in his presence.

Flexibility is another instrumentation issue to which observational researchers are keenly sensitive. Whereas the survey researcher can simply schedule mailings or phone calls, the ethnographer's schedule is determined by the field setting of her or his research. Unanticipated events can change the observational schedule or location at any time, and ethnographers must be flexible enough to adapt on short notice. To facilitate this, they will often work hard to cultivate relationships with key people who will notify them of important events as they occur.

Sudnow had to be very flexible in order to be present immediately after a patient died. He witnessed encounters between doctors and the family members of deceased patients and listened in on telephone announcements of patients' deaths. One way that he was able to unobtrusively witness face-to-face encounters was by posing as a doctor in hospital attire. He gained access to phone conversations by making arrangements with physicians to contact him prior to making the calls. Sudnow was so ever-present during these encounters that in some instances he became familiar enough with grieving family members to tag along with them as they left the hospital. These opportunities were critical to Sudnow's analysis of "the problems of interactions between bereaved and non-bereaved people in our society" (1967, p. 11). His availability to observe at crucial moments became a major factor in his ability to conduct such an intensive analysis. Had his flexibility been limited by external scheduling demands, he could not have served so effectively as a research instrument.

To stay objective while recording interactions and conversations is another challenge for the ethnographer. To what extent can researchers remove the blinders of bias and report the social world from the viewpoint of the participants under observation? Not only can these blinders affect the way observations are interpreted but also researchers' determinations of what activity is worth observing. Sudnow wrestled with these issues in his self-expository discussion of "descriptive bias" (1967, p.176); because he was an outsider in the world of medicine, his choices of interpretations and observational events were greatly affected by his own biases and interests. Sudnow views this distinction as an insurmountable limitation to ethnographic research:

> Being practically involved in the world of medicine and nursing places a perspective around events which no outsider can hope fully to achieve, short of becoming a physician or nurse himself. I can claim only a limited insight into the cognitive life of the medical world, and while some of the considerations which I feel govern work in that world have been stated, there is much which I feel remains inaccessible to the ethnographer. (1967, p. 176)

Sudnow also challenges the ability of researchers to maintain objectivity in their recognition of "facts." As an example from his own research, he cites an analytical point made in his book concerning the lack of privacy afforded patients at the charity hospital. Supporting evidence revealed the "fact" that the sheets used in the public ward did not always completely cover the patients' bodies; as a result, their genitals were often exposed. Sudnow's "middle-class" bias made him quite concerned about this loss of privacy, so he assumed that nurses and doctors, typically from middle-class backgrounds themselves, would have the same reaction. But he could not assume that the primarily lower-class patients of this hospital would be equally concerned about their privacy.

Sudnow, therefore, had to struggle with the question of whether or not lack of privacy constituted a "fact" if its importance was not universally recognized. This would be particularly relevant if the patients themselves, as well as their visitors, did not object to the exposure of their private parts. This attitudinal question directly challenged instrumentation that rely on human senses. Nevertheless, Sudnow concluded that his observations, although affected by bias, were still pertinent to the social treatment of death and dying in a medical context.

ASSESSMENT QUESTIONS
for *Research Brief,* Chapter 5

*Name*_____*Date*_____

Answer the following questions in relation to the research brief just presented:

1. Discuss how our social class values might limit the usefulness of "common sense" in collecting ethnographic data.

2. To what extent do you agree with Sudnow's conclusion that ethnographers' insights into their research are inevitably limited simply because they are not true participants?

   Discuss your response.

3. Assess Sudnow's strategies for becoming a "fly on the wall" as a non-participant observer.

4. List three strategies that you might develop to minimize your presence as a non-participant observer in a study of a government agency's treatment of the public.

1)

2)

3)

5. Flexibility is an important aspect of instrumentation for ethnographic research due to

    a.   the need to adjust your observations to schedules set by others.
    b.   the need to interpret data in multiple ways.
    c.   the requirement that researchers minimize their presence.
    d.   all of the above.
    e.   none of the above.

6. What was Sudnow's primary research instrument?

    a.   a structured survey
    b.   hospital documents
    c.   observational capabilities
    d.   an in-depth interview protocol

Chapter 5

Tools and Data:
The First Draft

Name_____Date_____

A student came to us requesting feedback on a questionnaire she was preparing for her senior thesis research. She had selected the general topic of adoption. Specifically, her research questions involved adoptees' attitudes and feelings about having been adopted, their treatment as adopted children, and whether they were engaged in any search for their birth parents.

Below, you will find some of the items from the first draft of her survey instrument. Read each item, identify the problem(s), then revise the item to improve it (them).

1. As a child, did you ever discuss your adoption with anyone?

   Yes or no: _____

   If yes, what was their response? Please check the appropriate space:

   It made no difference to them: _____
   They thought it was great: _____
   They thought it was awful: _____

   Problem(s):

   Revision:

2. Was the "Chosen Baby" story used to help you understand what it means to be adopted? (yes, no or don't know):

Problem(s):

Revision:

3. Did your adoptive family try to keep your adoption secret? Please answer yes or no to the following:

    a.   From you?   _____
    b.   From relatives?   _____
    c.   From friends and neighbors?   _____

Problem(s):

Revision:

4. Were your adoptive parents/family supportive of your search? How so?

Problem(s):

Revision:

5. Have you ever sought out any non-identifying information regarding your birth parents?

Problem(s):

Revision:

6. Would you ever or have you ever given up a child for adoption? Why or why not?

Problem(s):

Revision:

7. If you decided to adopt a child, would there be anything from your experience as an adoptee that would enable you or make you reconsider the way in which you would raise this child and, perhaps, educate him or her about what it means to be adopted?

Problem(s):

Revision:

8. What is your adoptive parents' educational level?

Problem(s):

Revision:

Chapter 5

Application:
Guttman Scale

Name_____Date_____

This exercise will provide you with an opportunity to see how a Guttman scale is developed. The topic will be attitude toward drinking behavior, from which some potential items have been selected that could be included in the scale. You will be asked to choose four items and test them among a sample of respondents. Then you must analyze the results according to procedures typically used in the development of a Guttman Scale. Begin with this list of situations in which people might drink alcohol:

- Studying for an exam
- About to drive a car
- During working hours
- About to attend a routine class
- On a casual date during the weekend
- At a New Year's Eve party
- At a bar with friends
- About to take an important exam
- About to go on an important job interview

Review this list to consider how to formulate a Guttman Scale which could measure attitudes toward drinking behavior. The introduction to the scale would read as follows:

Listed below are situations in which people sometimes find themselves. For each one, place a check next to the number if you believe it is acceptable to drink alcohol in that situation. Your responses will remain confidential.

Next, select four items for your scale. These items should differ from each other in their level of intensity, i.e., the percentage of expected acceptance of drinking for each situation. (In other words, choose situations which you predict will produce different responses.) The item with the greatest percentage of acceptance should be listed first, the second highest percentage next, the third next, and least percentage last. These will represent your "predicted response patterns."

Create your scale on the following page (Drinking Situation Survey) by entering the items which you select. Make ten copies of your scale and submit it to ten people. After the surveys are completed, give each person an identification code by numbering each survey from one to ten at the top of the page.

Evaluate the response pattern which you obtained by recording your results on the evaluation sheet provided on page 66. Analyze these results in the questions which follow.

DRINKING SITUATION SURVEY

Listed below are situations in which people sometimes find themselves. For each one, place a check next to the number if you believe it is acceptable to drink alcohol in that situation. Your responses will remain confidential.

_____1.

_____2.

_____3.

_____4.

Thank you for your cooperation.

EVALUATION OF DRINKING SITUATION SURVEY

I. Beginning with respondent #1, place a plus sign (+) under each item which the respondent checked and a minus sign (-) under each item that was left blank. Repeat this procedure for the remaining nine respondents.

Response Pattern:

Respondent #	Item			
	1	2	3	4
1.	——	——	——	——
2.	——	——	——	——
3.	——	——	——	——
4.	——	——	——	——
5.	——	——	——	——
6.	——	——	——	——
7.	——	——	——	——
8.	——	——	——	——
9.	——	——	——	——
10.	——	——	——	——

II. Record the number of predicted response patterns that resulted from your sample. (Predicted patterns rank logically and consistently along a continuum.)

Predicted Pattern   Number of Cases

+ + + +   ___

+ + + -   ___

+ + - -   ___

+ - - -   ___

- - - -   ___

Note any alternative response patterns, e.g., + - + -, - - + +, or - + + -, and the number of cases for each one. (Hint: Alternative response patterns always involve a negative sign preceding a positive sign.)

Pattern   Number of Cases

                            ___

                            ___

                            ___

                            ___

                            ___

III. Analyze your results by responding to the following questions:

A. How many people responded in your predicted pattern?

___Number   ___Percent of your sample

B. Calculate a coefficient of reproducibility by using the following formula:

$$1 - \frac{\text{(Number of alternative patterns)}}{\begin{array}{l}\text{Number of cases x} \\ \text{Number of scale items}\end{array}}$$

Coefficient = ___   (This item reflects the percentage of correct predictions.)

C. Are you confident that this set of situations creates a Guttman scale?

___ Yes ___ No

Discuss your response based on the information reported in B and C above.

D. Are there any common alternative response patterns which might suggest revisions which would improve the scale? Discuss.

How else might you explain your results?

Chapter 6

How Do We Deal with the Inevitable Error? Validity and Reliability

✓ *Research Brief:*

A Researcher's Nightmare

✓ *Tools and Data:*

Does Getting to Know Your Sample Help?

✓ *Application:*

Testing for Validity and Reliability
in a Crisis Situation

Chapter 6

Research Brief:
A Researcher's Nightmare

"Hello, Principal [Rodriguez]. This is [Lindsay Powell] from Educational Research, Inc.* I have just experienced a researcher's nightmare and I need to ask for your assistance and understanding in order to correct the problem (Powell, 1991)."

This phone call was made to over 60 school principals in 1990 to rectify an error which almost invalidated a carefully crafted research design. The study design was a pretest/posttest quasi-experimental evaluation of a program to help at-risk students. Three to four member teams from 100 schools across the state were trained in instructional strategies to promote mainstreaming of students who would otherwise attend special and compensatory-education classes. After completing two training sessions, the teams were expected to train the rest of their school staffs in the programs and techniques they had learned.

Educational Research, Inc. had been contracted to evaluate the effectiveness of the team-training approach. A pretest questionnaire, to be used during the pretraining period, provided questions about the skills and knowledge of the team members prior to the training. The posttest instrument, to be administered after the training, posed similar questions to determine whether there was any change in the participants' knowledge and skills as a result of the training.

Powell had established *face validity* of the instruments by discussing the questionnaire items with an advisory board of educational experts. The board recommended changes in approximately two-thirds of the questions to improve their clarity. For example, a scale item in the first draft which stated, "I know how to solicit the views of school personnel to ensure that everyone has input in important decisions affecting the entire school" was simplified to read, "I know how to make sure everyone in the school has input in important decisions affecting the entire school."

---

*Pseudonyms are used to protect the identities of the participants.

The questionnaire was revised shortly before the training sessions began. Sessions were scheduled to begin at different times for each of the five groups with an interval of a few weeks between the first and second sessions. Powell sent out the revised questionnaire to the first group of trainees and shortly thereafter left on vacation. Upon her return, she was pleased to discover that, in her absence, her secretary had distributed pretest questionnaires to three of the remaining groups. When the questionnaires were returned, however, it became apparent that groups two through four had been sent the original, unrevised version.

This mistake created a serious problem. Since the groups had responded to two different questionnaires, their scores could not be compared. In addition, the earlier draft had significant problems with its face validity. Powell had never before encountered a situation like this; nothing in her education or training had prepared her for such an eventuality. She thought of resigning so that the research company could save face by using her as a "fall guy," but she enjoyed her position as a research scientist and did not really want to resign. Instead, she took a deep breath, contemplated the situation, and consulted with the research director about remedial strategies.

After thinking through various options, Powell and the research director decided that Powell would personally telephone the principals of the 60 schools that had received incorrect questionnaires to explain the situation and request their help. The building teams at these schools would be asked to complete a revised pretest regarding their knowledge and skills prior to having received the training. (These individuals had attended only one of the two sessions that comprised their training.) Answers from these groups would be compared to the responses from the first group to determine whether they differed significantly.

Most of the participants completed the new version of the pretest, although approximately ten percent of the sample—about 40 people—refused. A comparison of the first group's answers with those of groups two through four showed similar response patterns. It did not seem to matter that the middle groups' responses were based on their memories of their prior knowledge and skills. These results assured Powell and her colleagues that, although the lack of standardization in the pretest data collection process could have reduced the validity and reliability of their study, the evaluation would still prove useful as a way of measuring the effects of the training.

ASSESSMENT QUESTIONS
for *Research Brief,* Chapter 6

*Name*_____*Date*_____

Answer the following questions relating to the research brief just presented.

1. How well do you think the researchers corrected the pretest mix-up? Discuss.

2. What might you have done differently in the same situation?

3. Do you think that human subjects can accurately recall their knowledge and skills prior to participation in a training course? Why or why not?

4. Which of the following types of validity might have been jeopardized by the pretest mix-up? (Circle all that apply.)

   a. face
   b. content
   c. construct
   d. predictive

5. Which of the following reliability issues are relevant to the pretest mix-up? (Circle all that apply.)

   a. Different coders may have differed in their judgments of open-ended questionnaire items.
   b. Respondents may have answered differently in the top half of the pretest than the bottom half.
   c. Respondents from different groups completed the questionnaires under different circumstances.
   d. Respondents may have provided different information to the same questions between the first and second time.

Chapter 6

Tools and Data:
Does Getting to Know
Your Sample Help?

Researcher Kathleen Ferraro (1983) conducted participant observation research for ten months during 1978 and 1979 at a shelter for battered women in the southwestern part of the United States. During this period, 120 women with 165 children stayed at the shelter. In addition to engaging in daily interactions with and first-hand observations of the women, Ferraro conducted in-depth taped interviews with 10 residents and 5 other battered women not residing at the shelter.

Ferraro's research question had to do with how some women experience abusive relationships. She was particularly interested in this topic, since she herself had been a battered woman.

From her observations and interviews, Ferraro determined six catalysts which enable women to view themselves as victims and to finally leave their abusive situation: "(1) a change in the level of violence, (2) a change in resources, (3) a change in the relationship, (4) despair, (5) a change in the visibility of violence, and (6) external definitions of the relationship" (p. 326).

Excerpts from Ferraro's interviews which apply to each type of catalyst are presented below:

(1) A change in the level of violence:

It was like a pendulum. He'd swing to the extremes both ways. He'd get drunk and beat me up, then he'd get sober and treat me like a queen. One day he put a gun to my head and pulled the trigger. It wasn't loaded. But that's when I decided I'd had it. I sued for separation of property. I knew what was coming again, so I got out. I didn't want to. I still loved the guy, but I knew I had to for my own sanity.

(2) A change in resources:

I stayed with him because I didn't want my kids to have the same life I did. My parents were divorced, and I was always so ashamed of that. . . . Yes, they're all on their own now, so there's no reason left to stay.

Of course, another obvious change in resources is in the availability of shelters which offer a woman who leaves an abusive situation a place to go.

(3) A change in the relationship:

At first, you know, we used to have so much fun together. He has kind've, you know, a magnetic personality; he can be really charming. But it isn't fun anymore. Since the baby came, it's changed completely. He just wants me to stay at home, while he goes out with his friends. He doesn't even talk to me, most of the time. . . . No, I don't really love him anymore, not like I did.

(4) Despair:

Before the Al-Anon program can really be of benefit, a woman has to hit bottom. When you hit bottom, you realize that all of your own efforts to control the situation have failed; you feel helpless and lost and worthless and completely disenchanted with the world. Women can't really be helped unless they're ready for it and want it. Some women come here when things get bad, but they aren't really ready to be committed to Al-Anon. Things haven't gotten bad enough for them, and they go right back. We see this all the time. [Director of an Al-Anon organized shelter]

(5) A change in the visibility of violence:

He never hit me in public before—it was always at home. But the Saturday I got back [returned to her husband from the shelter], we went Christmas shopping and he slapped me in the store because of some stupid joke I made. People saw it, I know, I felt so stupid, like, they must all think what a jerk I am, what a sick couple, and I thought, "God, I must be crazy to let him do this."

(6) External definitions of the relationship:

My mother-in-law knew what was going on, but she wouldn't admit it. . . . I said, "Mom, what do you think these bruises are?" and she said "Well, some people just bruise easy. I do it all the time, bumping into things". . . . And he just denied it, pretended like nothing happened, and if I'd said I wanted to talk about it, he'd say, "Life goes on, you can't just dwell on things". . . . But this time, my neighbor knew what happened, she saw it, and when he denied it, she said, "I can't believe it! You know that's not true!". . . . And I was so happy that finally somebody else saw what was goin' on, and I just told him then that this time I wasn't gonna' come home!

According to Ferraro, shelters for battered women are too understaffed to conduct systematic follow-ups (beyond a month or two) of residents after they leave. However, she was able to follow the women in her study through their post-shelter experience due to the personal relationships she had developed with them. She learned that 30 of the 120 women had been "successful" in achieving self-confidence, positive relationships with others, and optimism about their future. Thirty others had on-going severe problems, even though they had not returned to their abusive relationships. The remaining 60 (50 percent) had returned to their previous relationships.

ASSESSMENT QUESTIONS
for *Tools and Data,* Chapter 6

Name_____Date_____

Answer the following questions pertaining to Ferraro's study of residents at a shelter for battered women.

1. Which of the following could have been particularly important in establishing validity?
    a. Ferraro developed sympathy for the women.
    b. Ferraro was able to observe the women's interactions with their children.
    c. The research was conducted over a period of several months.
    d. The participation-observation method of collecting data enabled Ferraro to develop a first-hand understanding of the women's decisions to leave their abusive partners.

2. What problem associated with bias might have affected the validity of the findings in this study?
    a. The researcher did not administer unbiased closed-ended questionnaires.
    b. The researcher was unable to get to know the women as individuals.
    c. The sample was made up almost entirely of women who had already left their abusers.
    d. Most of the women in the sample had negative attitudes toward men.

3. What could be a problem with establishing reliability in a study such as this?
    a. The lack of standardization in data-gathering instruments, i.e., closed-ended questions on a questionnaire.
    b. The lack of follow up with the women after they left the shelter.
    c. The limitation of the study to one region of the country.
    d. The failure to interview the women's abusers.

4. What are two things that could be done to increase the likelihood of establishing validity of the findings in this study? (Example: Ask the women about their understanding of what it means to be in an abusive relationship.)

   a.

   b.

5. What are two things that could be done to increase the likelihood of establishing reliability of the findings in this study? (Example: Conduct some of the interviews away from the shelter.)

   a.

   b.

6. Develop two probes for catalyst #3 which would clarify how the relationship had changed.

   a.

   b.

7. Develop two coding criteria to clearly distinguish between catalyst #1—a change in the level of violence—and catalyst #3—a change in the relationship.

   a.

   b.

Chapter 6

Application:
Testing for Validity and Reliability
In a Crisis Situation

Name_____Date_____

Imagine that you are involved in a research study on how families of AIDS sufferers cope with the crisis. The study will use both survey and field methods of collecting data to ensure validity and reliability. The survey part of the study will entail administering questionnaires to a sample of the family members of participants in a medical study of AIDS patients at a large hospital. The field part of the study will involve in-depth interviews with a smaller subsample of family members and observation in their homes and during hospital visits with their AIDS-stricken relatives over a period of several weeks. Overall, the research team expects that there will be a high degree of emotion exhibited by the family members.

Answer the following questions pertaining to this study.

1. For which part of the study (survey or field) would it be easier to establish validity?

   Why?

2. For which part of the study (survey or field) would it be easier to establish reliability?

   Why?

3. Describe how you might go about establishing face validity.

4. Describe how you might go about establishing construct validity.

5. Suggest two ways you might go about establishing reliability.

   a.

   b.

Chapter 7

How Many?
The Science and Art
of Sampling

✔ *Research Brief:*

Getting Beyond the White and
Middle-Class Experience

✔ *Tools and Data:*

'Hello, This Is City Hall Calling'

✔ *Application:*

Sampling

Chapter 7

Research Brief:
Getting Beyond the White and Middle-Class Experience

Researchers who set out to obtain racially and socially diverse samples may have to adjust their design decisions in order to achieve their goals. Consider, for example, the experience of Lynn Weber Cannon and her colleagues, Elizabeth Higginbotham and Marianne L.A. Leung (1988) in their study of the general mental health and well-being of women employed in middle-class occupations. The research focused on the effects of race, class, and gender inequality, so it was imperative that their sample represented diverse populations.

The study methodology was of a qualitative design using two- to three-hour, face-to-face, life-history interviews. Women born between 1945 and 1960 were targeted because of the availability of funds to help working-class and black women attend college during that period. The researchers sought participants who were college graduates employed full-time in professional, administrative, and managerial positions in the United States.

The researchers faced two sampling challenges. There were no official lists organized by race and class of women employed in various middle-class positions. In addition, the study methodology of lengthy, face-to-face, life-history interviews could impede the recruitment of participants due to the commitment of time required and the personal nature of the interviews.

The sampling method selected was a quota design, which stratified participants according to the variables of race, class, gender composition of the occupation (male- versus female-dominated), professionals versus managers and administrators, specific occupation, and age category. Volunteers who met the requirements were to be randomly selected each week for participation in the study.

The researchers used standard recruitment strategies such as letters to professional and social organizations, letters to women identified as prospective volunteers, and announcements in the local media describing the study and requesting volunteers. Women who were interested received a personal letter and a description of the recruitment criteria. Those with continued interest were asked to complete a one-page form.

This approach was effective in recruiting participants who met the researchers' recruitment goal of diversity in social-class origin. Women of both middle- and working-class origins responded fairly evenly. The goal of racial diversity was not achieved, however, since far more white than black women responded. The initial recruitment effort produced only 38.8 percent of the black participants compared to 74.1 percent of the white participants.

The researchers reassessed their recruitment strategies and decided to use more labor-intensive methods, such as presentations at meetings and word-of-mouth snowball techniques. This modification provided much better results. Nine months of recruitment efforts produced a sample of 400 women which was approximately one-third black and two-thirds white, a rate consistent with or slightly higher than the regional representation.

The researchers identified three plausible explanations for the success of these new strategies:

First, they surmised that black women were more skeptical about the purpose of the research than were white women. Over time, some minority-group members have come to suspect that participation in a study may result in exploitation. While white women felt comfortable about participating because of the information they obtained from letters or media stories, black women were more likely to require personal contact to assure them that the study would not exploit them or others.

Second, the researchers concluded that black women needed greater assurances of anonymity than white women, particularly those who held such high-visibility positions as vice presidents, newscasters, and judges. Their comparatively small numbers in such positions increased the likelihood that their interview responses could be attributed to specific individuals. Here again, personal contact strategies enabled researchers to offer the black women additional assurances of guaranteed anonymity.

Third, the black women generally experienced greater structural barriers to their participation, such as less free time, than did the white women. There were more scheduling problems due to the limited availability of time and more cancellations due to unforeseen circumstances among the black women than among the white women during the course of the interviews. This difference, as well as the lower volunteer rates among black women, may be at least partially attributed to the higher incidence of black women with the dual role of employee and parent.

Despite comparable marital statuses between races, two-thirds of the black women had children in contrast to only one-third of the white women.

Although samples may be restricted for research, cost, or political reasons, most biased samples are accidental. Nevertheless, they still detract from the generalizability of the research. Cannon, Higginbotham and Leung argue that their experience provides an important lesson in sampling because they successfully met the recruitment goals of racial and class-origin diversity through the use of labor-intensive recruitment strategies that differed from those typically employed. By developing sampling techniques that are specifically adapted to their target participants, researchers can help ensure that our understanding of "social realities" (1988, p. 460) will not be limited to the white and middle-class world.

ASSESSMENT QUESTIONS
for *Research Brief,* Chapter 7

*Name*_____*Date*_____

Answer the following questions in regards to the research brief just presented.

1. Name three ways that the researchers' original recruitment strategies created a sampling bias.

    a.

    b.

    c.

2. Identify two other types of recruitment strategies that the researchers might have used in order to obtain diversity in race and social class.

    a.

    b.

3. Why, in your opinion, did the researchers use non-probability sampling rather than probability sampling in their study?

4. Which of the following units best describes the sampling unit for this study?

   a. households
   b. workplaces
   c. women employed in middle-class occupations
   d. professionals

5. Which sampling method best describes the method used in this study?

   a. multistage cluster
   b. stratified
   c. systematic
   d. quota

Chapter 7

Tools and Data:
'Hello, This Is City Hall Calling'

Many cities have undergone major redevelopment of their downtown areas in recent years. Development plans typically include the rebuilding of a retail core and the renovating or demolishing of dilapidated buildings that house low-income people. Usually, public meetings are held to allow the public to comment on the plans.

Some local governments, however, survey their residents in order to collect data systematically for the planning process. Such surveys are usually conducted on a sample of the population rather than the population as a whole. Therefore, the city must first select a specific sampling method.

Each sampling method has advantages and disadvantages in terms of ease of implementation, precision, and costs. Four methods were directly compared in Conduit's computerized simulation entitled SAMP: Survey Sampling (1981).* These methods were (1) simple random, (2) cluster, (3) stratified, and (4) quota.

The simple random method used voter registration lists for its frame, while the cluster method used only a proportion of those lists. A combination of voter registration lists and property tax assessment records became the frame for the stratified method. No frame was used for the quota method, however, because it was not based on probability.

Table 1 compares the precision of responses to an attitudinal question about downtown redevelopment, using the four different methods. This comparison is possible because the values for the entire population are available within the SAMP computer simulation. The attitude values range from one—strongly against—to five—strongly in favor. The mean score for the population is 3.172; the standard deviation is 1.654.

---

*A computer program which estimates the values for the variables being studied under various conditions. These estimations make it possible to create different hypothetical scenarios and outcomes for the scenarios.

Table 1. Precision of Results with Four Contrasting Sampling Methods[1]

Method	Mean Attitude Score	Standard Deviation	Standard Error[2]
Simple Random	3.12	1.685	.144
Cluster[3]	3.438	1.592	.520
Stratified[4]	3.170	1.611	.114
Quota[5]	3.084	1.652	—

[1]Sample size constitutes five percent of the population.
[2]95 percent confidence level.
[3]10 clusters
[4]Stratified by tax-assessed values of respondents' houses into three groups: rich, middle class, and poor,
[5]Quotas were established by age and sex.

Ease of implementation is determined based on the total number of interviews required, the number of call-backs (follow-up phone calls), and the distance traveled between interviews. Comparative data for these four methods are provided in Table 2.

Table 2. Ease of Implementation with Four Contrasting Sampling Methods

Method	Sampling Frame	# Interviews	# Callbacks	Mean Distance Between Interviews (Miles)
Simple Random	Voter Registration Lists	552	230	1.285
Cluster	Appropriate Proportion of Voter Registration Lists	555	193	.200
Stratified	Voter Registration Lists and Property Tax Assessment Records	553	186	1.244
Quota	None	550	0	.015

Since research takes place in a budgetary context, cost is an important consideration in research decisions. Table 3 allows us to see the expenses that each method entails.

Table 3. Costs for Four Contrasting Sampling Methods (in Dollars)

Method	Acquiring Frame[1]	Selecting Sample[2]	Travel Expenses[3]	Wages While Traveling[4]	Wages While Interviewing[5]	Wages for Call-back[6]	Total Cost[7]
Simple Random	125.00	60.00	500.00	427.50	690.00	97.50	1,900.00
Cluster	62.50	30.00	75.00	62.50	695.00	82.50	1,007.50
Stratified	250.00	120.00	460.00	·390.00	692.50	80.00	1,992.50
Quota	0	0	0	235.00[8]	687.50	0	992.50

[1]$125 x number of lists
[2]$60 x number of lists (or proportion of list)
[3]$0.50 x (# of interviews + # of call-backs) x mean distance between interviews
[4]$0.425 x (# of interviews + # of call-backs) x mean distance between interviews
[5]$1.25 x # of interviews
[6]$0.425 x # of call-backs
[7]Sum of items 1 through 6
[8]Cost of wages while finding respondents = $0.425 x # of interviews

This simulated comparison provides a detailed view of the advantages and disadvantages of different sampling methods. Of course, these particular findings were affected by specific research conditions, such as a bimodal data distribution and relatively little travel distance (compared to national studies). As research conditions change, so should research decisions.

EXERCISE
for *Tools and Data,* Chapter 7

*Name*_____*Date*_____

Answer the following questions pertaining to the preceding comparison of sampling methods.

1. Which sampling method offered the greatest precision?

    a. simple random
    b. cluster
    c. stratified
    d. quota

2. Which sampling method was the easiest to implement in terms of the least number of call-backs as well as the least mean distance traveled between interviews?

    a. simple random
    b. cluster
    c. stratified
    d. quota

3. Which sampling method was the least expensive to implement?

    a. simple random
    b. cluster
    c. stratified
    d. quota

4. Which sampling method carries the greatest risk of producing biased data?

    a. simple random
    b. cluster
    c. stratified
    d. quota

Why did you select this/these method(s)?

5. Which method would you recommend for this survey, based on the data provided?

   a. simple random
   b. cluster
   c. stratified
   d. quota

Why did you select this method?

Chapter 7

Application:
Sampling

Name_____Date_____

Develop a brief questionnaire to collect demographic data on the following characteristics:

(1) Sex
(2) Year in college, i.e., freshman, sophomore, junior, senior, or graduate student

Select a small group of people on campus (about 20 to 50 people) which you can easily contact, e.g., a class, club, or dormitory wing. Administer your questionnaire to each individual in this group.

Record the total numbers and convert them to percentages in the tables below:

Sex:

	Male	Female
Total number	____	____
Percentage	____	____

College Year:

	Freshman	Sophomore	Junior	Senior	Graduate
Total number	____	____	____	____	____
Percentage	____	____	____	____	____

2. Collect the same demographic data in aggregate form (totals and percentages) for the entire student body from an official campus source, e.g., registrar, admission office, or student housing. For example, find out the percent distribution for both males and females in the student body. Record that information in the tables below:

Sex:

	Male	Female
Total number	_____	_____
Percentage	_____	_____

College Year:

	Freshman	Sophomore	Junior	Senior	Graduate
Total number	_____	_____	_____	_____	_____
Percentage	_____	_____	_____	_____	_____

3. Analyze the extent to which your sample (college group) is representative of the overall college population. Address the following questions:

   a. How do the percent distributions compare for both sex and college year? Provide an explanation for the results of this comparison.

      Sex:

      College Year:

      Explanation:

   b. Identify a campus group(s) which might be a more representative sample of the student body in terms of sex and year in school.

      Campus Group:

Discuss why you believe this group might be more representative than the group which you had selected.

c. What sampling method would you recommend for obtaining a representative sample (e.g., cluster, stratified, accidental)?

Method:

Why did you select this method?

d. What are two potential limitations of the method which you selected?

1)

2)

Chapter 8

'This Will Just Take A Few Minutes of Your Time': Surveys

✓ **Research Brief:**

A New Look at the Effects of Divorce on Children

✓ **Tools and Data:**

Survey Preparation

✓ **Applications:**

1. Survey Administration – Method Effectiveness
2. Survey Administration – Interviewer Bias

Chapter 8

Research Brief:
A New Look at the Effects of Divorce on Children

The effects of divorce on children are a serious concern. Research literature documents differences between children of divorced parents and children from two-parent families, including more emotional problems, more behavioral problems, and lower scholastic achievement among children of divorced parents (Cherlin, et al., 1991). Most of these studies are based on observational research strategies with non-random and relatively small samples.

Andrew Cherlin and his colleagues (1991) believed that additional research strategies were needed to further our understanding of the effects of divorce. Particularly interested in determining why children of divorced parents do less well, they designed their research to examine this question using a longitudinal survey approach. This approach would lend itself to studying larger numbers of children than is usually possible in observational designs. The longitudinal element would allow them to follow the children in their study over time to better understand why the divorce effects occur.

Cherlin's group took advantage of two existing survey sources to accomplish their research. The first survey, National Child Development Study (NCDS), conducted in Great Britain at various times, focused on the study of perinatal mortality. Nearly all women giving birth (98 percent) in England, Scotland, and Wales in 1958 were interviewed, and 85 percent of these mothers were successfully re-interviewed in 1965 when their children reached 7 years of age. The surveys, administered by trained nurses, were comprised mostly of behavioral questions in the Rutter Home Behavior Scale. Teachers of the 7-year-old children also participated by filling out the Bristol Social Adjustment Guide (BSAG). The children themselves completed reading and math tests and physical exams. Similar data were collected in 1969 when the children reached age 11.

The second existing survey was the National Survey of Children (NSC) conducted in the United States in both 1976 and 1981. The 1976 survey included a random sample of 2,279 children between the ages of 7 and 11. The 1981 follow-up surveyed children from the original sample whose parents had separated, divorced, or were having severe marital conflict in 1976, as well as a randomly selected subsample of children whose families were intact and not experiencing conflict at that time. The survey questions in both stages of data collection were asked of the parents, typically the mother. The behavioral questions were similar to the ones in the British study. Parents were also asked about any conflict with their spouses in 1976.

The British survey data were analyzed first. The U.S. data were examined to help determine the generalizability of the British results.

The British data showed both expected and unexpected findings. As expected, the children whose parents divorced or separated during the previous 5 years had significantly greater behavioral problems at age 11 than children from intact families. Reading and mathematics scores were also significantly lower for children of divorced or separated parents. The researchers accounted for social class and race as "control variables" in their analysis, but the findings held up regardless of the influence of either of these factors.

The research further provided an important unexpected finding. Using information about the children at age 7 as "control variables," the researchers showed that differences between children from intact families and those from divorced or separated families began *prior* to the divorce or separation. This finding occurred for boys in both achievement and behavioral outcomes, and for girls in achievement only.

In the U.S. survey, as in the British survey, boys whose parents divorced or separated between 1976 and 1981 had more behavioral problems than did boys living with both biological parents. (Achievement outcomes were not tested because comparable achievement data were not available.) Also, like the British data, the U.S. study showed that these differences diminished when behavioral problems already existing in 1976 were included in the analysis. Surprisingly, contrary findings occurred for girls. No differences in behavioral problems were evident between girls from intact families and girls whose parents were separated or divorced, and when 1976 behavioral problems were considered in the analysis, girls whose parents separated or divorced had even fewer behavioral problems than those whose families remained intact.

These research results suggest the possibility that marital conflict, rather than divorce or separation, is the actual cause of children's behavioral problems. The researchers recommend, therefore, that those interested in the effects of divorce on children regard such conflict as a matter for serious attention and concern.

ASSESSMENT QUESTIONS
for *Research Brief,* Chapter 8

*Name*_____*Date*_____

Answer the following questions in relation to the research brief just presented:

1. Construct two hypotheses for testing the relevance of marital conflict on behavioral outcomes.

    (1)

    (2)

2. Construct a brief introduction (about one paragraph long) to a new survey concerning the relationship between marital conflict and behavioral outcomes.

3. Consider the challenge of human subjects in administering surveys to study the effects of divorce. List two risks to human subjects which such a survey might entail.

    (1)

    (2)

4. How did the longitudinal element of this research design improve our understanding of the effects of divorce?

    a. It helped ensure that people answered similarly from one time period to the next.
    b. It provided time for behavioral or achievement problems to work themselves out.
    c. It provided an opportunity to examine behavioral and achievement variables preceding divorce or separation.
    d. It allowed a larger sample to be included in the research.

5. The decreased participation in the British study may have produced a response bias. Which of the following forms of bias might be present?

    a. People who moved may be under-represented because they were difficult to locate.
    b. The respondents may be skewed toward families which remained intact because separated or divorced parents may have refused to participate.
    c   The respondents may be skewed toward families who trusted nurses, because nurses administered the surveys.
    d. None of the above.
    e. All of the above.

Chapter 8

 Tools and Data:
Survey Preparation

Imagine that you have been commissioned by your city to conduct a study on homeless people in the metropolitan area. Government leaders are particularly interested in attitudes held by the homeless because they intend to develop policies or programs to reduce the incidence of homelessness. A city staff person suggests that you include the following questions as part of your questionnaire:

1. When did you decide that you were a homeless person?

2. When did you leave your wife behind?

3. Don't you think you would feel better if you had a job?

    ___ Yes
    ___ No
    ___ Undecided

4. Do you think it is fair to panhandle from hard-working people?

    ___ Yes
    ___ No
    ___ Undecided

5. Do you expect the government or charities to support you indefinitely?

    ___ Yes
    ___ No
    ___ Undecided

*Name*_____*Date*_____

Each survey question suggested by the city staff member has a technical problem, such as being double-barreled, leading, or biased. Therefore, it is important to determine what information the staff person is seeking, i.e., the intent of each question, and to revise the questions accordingly.

This exercise involves the following steps:

- Identify the variable which the question is intended to measure, e.g., attitude toward violence.
- Identify potential technical or bias problems for each question.
- Rewrite each question with more appropriate wording. It may be necessary to develop additional questions to eliminate bias or technical problems.

1. Variable:

   Problem(s):

   Revision:

2. Variable:

   Problem(s):

   Revision:

3. Variable:

   Problem(s):

   Revision:

4. Variable:

   Problem(s):

   Revision:

5. Variable:

   Problem(s):

   Revision:

Chapter 8

Applications:
1. Survey Administration – Method Effectiveness
2. Survey Administration – Interviewer Bias

Name_____Date_____

1. SURVEY ADMINISTRATION – METHOD EFFECTIVENESS

This exercise will compare in-person interviewing with telephone interviewing.

1. Develop three questions concerning a topical issue of your choice that is of sociological interest and somewhat controversial, and about which there would likely be a range of attitudes. Include two closed-ended questions and one open-ended question. Make sure that at least one question is likely to be difficult for respondents to answer, possibly causing some embarrassment or discomfort.

2. Develop one hypothesis regarding method effectiveness, i.e., which method— in-person or telephone interviewing—is likely to be more effective in obtaining data about the issue. The hypothesis should pertain to one of the following: relative ease of administration, ability to get truthful responses, comfort level, level of detail, or response rate.

3. Select two samples, each comprised of three respondents who are not your friends or family. They should have similar characteristics, e.g., are all college students, all about the same age, gender, etc., so that your results will not be greatly influenced by these variables.

4. Ask the three questions of each respondent separately, using contrasting methods: 1) an in-person interview, and 2) telephone interviewing of three respondents. Be sure to explain to each respondent that you are doing this for a class assignment and their responses will be confidential. Do not inform your respondents that you are doing something differently with another sample, as that information could affect the nature of their responses. Record their responses.

5. Provide answers to the items below.

    a. State your three questions (two closed-ended, one open-ended).

        1

        2.

        3.

    b. State your hypothesis.

    c. Describe your two samples and how you obtained them. Report any specific approach(es) that you implemented which helped your response rate.

        In-Person:

        Telephone:

        Approach(es):

    d. Summarize the responses from each sample.

        Closed-ended Question #1:

        In-Person Respondent: Telephone Respondent:

        1.   1.

        2.   2.

        3.   3.

        Summary of all responses (in percentages):

Closed-ended Question #2:

In-Person Respondent:	Telephone Respondent:
1.	1.
2.	2.
3.	3.

Summary of all responses (in percentages):

Open-ended Question:

In-Person Respondent:	Telephone Respondent:
1.	1.
2.	2.
3.	3.

Summary of all responses (in percentages):

e. Analyze the results in terms of your stated hypothesis, referring specifically to the response summaries above. Also discuss other observations that you made while conducting the two types of interviews about differences in method effectiveness (in terms of your comfort level, the comfort level of the respondents, which method seemed more effective in getting answers from respondents, and any difficulties with either or both).

2. SURVEY ADMINISTRATION – INTERVIEWER BIAS

This exercise involves examining possible differences in results based on interviewer bias, which may be present in one sample and not in the other.

1. Develop three questions concerning a topical issue of your choice that is of sociological interest and somewhat controversial, and about which there would likely be a range of attitudes. Include two closed-ended questions and one open-ended question. Make sure that at least one question is likely to be difficult for respondents to answer, possibly causing some embarrassment or discomfort.

2. Develop one hypothesis regarding the effect of interviewer bias, i.e., how the interviewer might or might not influence respondents' answers by displaying biases on the subject matter.

3. Select two samples, each comprised of three respondents who are not your friends or family. The respondents should have similar characteristics, e.g., all are college students, all about the same age, gender, etc., so that your results will not be greatly influenced by these variables.

4. Ask the three questions of each respondent personally and separately. Demonstrate your own bias(es) to the respondents in the first sample by indicating your opinions or attitudes and/or by acting enthusiastically or disapprovingly in response to their answers. Remain neutral and objective with the second group. Be sure to explain to each respondent that you are doing this for a class assignment and their responses will be confidential. Do not inform your respondents that you are doing something differently with another sample, as that information could affect the nature of their responses. Record their responses.

4. Provide answers to the items below.

   a. State your three questions (two closed-ended, one open-ended).

      1

      2.

      3.

b. State your hypothesis.

c. Describe your two samples and how you obtained them. Report any specific
    approach(es) that you implemented which helped your response rate.

    Interviewer Bias:

    Interviewer Neutrality:

    Approach(es):

d. Summarize the responses from each sample.
    Closed-ended Question #1:

    Biased Respondent: Neutral Respondent:

    1.   1.

    2.   2.

    3.   3.

    Summary of all responses (in percentages):

    Closed-ended Question #2:

    Biased Respondent: Neutral Respondent:
    1.   1.

2.   2.

3.   3.

Summary of all responses (in percentages):

Open-ended Question:
Biased Respondent: Neutral Respondent:

1.   1.

2.   2.

3.   3.

Summary of all responses (in percentages):

e. Analyze the results in terms of your stated hypothesis, referring specifically to the response summaries above. Also discuss other observations you made while conducting the two types of interviews, regarding differences in the influence of interviewer bias (in terms of your comfort level, the comfort level of the respondents, which seemed more effective in getting respondents to respond, and any difficulties with either or both).

Chapter 9

Where the Action Is: Field Research

✔ ***Research Brief:***

Being 'Inside and Outside'
as a Participant Observer

✔ ***Tools and Data:***

First Day on the Job

✔ ***Application:***

Field Research

Chapter 9

Research Brief:
Being 'Inside and Outside' as a Participant Observer

Sociological field research on American society can often parallel the anthropological studies of cultures in other societies. Occasionally the two may even coincide, as is the case in anthropologist Barbara Myerhoff's study in the 1970s of 300 elderly Jews within a senior citizens' center in the Venice Beach area of Southern California. During the four-year course of her research, she got to know and appreciate her subjects, most of whom had migrated from Eastern Europe and felt abandoned by their "successful" American-born children.

Initially, Myerhoff had concerns over her ability to be objective as a researcher, given that she herself was Jewish, that she was not elderly, and that this was a departure from the usual anthropological territory, such as a remote, exotic culture. In a book detailing her study, *Number Our Days* (1978, p. 18), she wrote about her attempts at objectivity:

> This is accomplished by attempting to experience the new culture from within, living in it for a time as a member, all the while maintaining sufficient detachment to observe and analyze it with some objectivity. This peculiar posture—being inside and outside at the same time—is called participant-observation. It is a fruitful paradox, one that has allowed anthropologists to find sense and purpose within a society's seemingly illogical and arbitrary customs and beliefs. This assumption of the natives' viewpoint, so to speak, is a means of knowing others through oneself, a professional technique that can be mastered fairly easily in the study of very different peoples. Working with one's own society and, more specifically, those of one's own ethnic and familial heritage, is perilous, and much more difficult. Yet it has a certain validity and value not available in other circumstances. Identifying with the 'Other'—Indians and Chicanos if one is Anglo, blacks if one is white, males if one is female—is an act of imagination, a means for discovering what one is not and will never be. Identifying with what one is now and will be someday is quite a different process.

There was also the matter of doing fieldwork on the elderly. She learned to

... .see old people now in a new way, as part of me, not "they." Most normal, relatively
sensitive people identify naturally with children. . . . But in our culture today, we do not
have this same natural attentiveness to and empathy with the elderly, in part because they
are not among us, and no doubt they are not among us because we don't want to recognize
the inevitability of our own future decline and dependence. (p. 19)

To better understand the physical feelings of the elderly comprising her sample,
Myerhoff tried out some "imaginative identification" by simulating being elderly,
". . .wearing stiff garden gloves to perform ordinary tasks, taking off my glasses and
plugging my ears, slowing down my movements and sometimes by wearing the heaviest
shoes I could find to their Center" (p. 18).

Myerhoff worked continuously with approximately half of the Center's members for
two years, then off and on for another two years. She came to know 80 of them
intimately and spent most of her time with 36 of them, visiting them in hospitals,
convalescent homes, and their own homes, taking trips with them outside their
neighborhoods, and attending their funerals. Ultimately she had to decide which ones
to use in the sample, since almost every one of the 300 wanted to be included.

The amount and variety of information accumulated in a field study is overwhelming. There
is no definite or correct solution to the problem of what to include, how to cut up the pie
of social reality, when precisely to leave or stop. Often there is little clarity as to whom to
include as 'members,' what to talk about with those who are. The deliberate avoidance of
preconceptions is likely to result in the best fieldwork, allowing the group or subject to
dictate the form the description ultimately takes. But always there is a high degree of
arbitrariness involved. Choices must be made and they are extremely difficult, primarily
because of what and who must be omitted. In this case, these methodological dilemmas
were especially troublesome. Nearly everyone at the Center wanted to be included, feeling
so strongly as they did the wish to be recorded and remembered.

Myerhoff also conducted "Living History" classes at the Center, which provided
another means for collecting data as well as a way to give something to the seniors.
She discussed how this came to be an important part of her study:

Center people, like so many of the elderly, were very fond of reminiscing and storytelling,
eager to be heard from, eager to relate parts of their life history. More afraid of oblivion
than pain or death, they always sought opportunities to become visible. Narrative activity
among them was intense and relentless. Age and proximity to death augmented the Jewish
predilection for verbal expression. In their stories, as in their cultural dramas, they
witnessed themselves, and thus knew who they were, serving as subject and object at once.
They narrated themselves perpetually, in the form of keeping notes, journals, writing poems
and reflections spontaneously, and also telling their stories to whomever would listen. Their
histories were not devoted to marking their successes or unusual merits. Rather they were
efforts at ordering, sorting, explaining—rendering coherent their long life, finding

integrating ideas and characteristics that helped them know themselves as the same person over time, despite great ruptures and shifts.

> . . . I was eager to respond to Center people's desires to tell me their stories and puzzled as to how to find the means and the time to listen to as many as possible. Abe [the Center Director] was helpful here, too. He suggested that I offer a class in the Center where people could assemble for recounting their life history. (pp. 33-34)

Myerhoff had to establish the class carefully. She wondered ". . . would people be willing to tell me, a stranger, their life history, and would they be inhibited if I tried to tape-record the sessions?" (p. 35).

The Director posted a sign: "New Center Class: Living History. Come and tell your story. Help teach our Professor Barbara about the beautiful life of the elderly. Tuesday at 10" (p. 35). After a month of advertising, Myerhoff began the classes, armed with refreshments, a tape recorder for class use, and notebooks and pencils for the participants to use at home. The longer the class continued, the more people attended and the more they had to say. Myerhoff "spoke as little as possible, occasionally focusing the topic or answering questions" (p. 36). What gradually emerged as the format was storytelling which, clearly, "was a passion among these people, absolutely central to their culture" (p. 37).

Thus developed an increasingly trusting relationship between Myerhoff and the members of her sample, which provided enjoyment for her subjects as well as a fruitful means of collecting data for her study.

ASSESSMENT QUESTIONS
for *Research Brief,* Chapter 9

Name_____Date_____

Answer the following questions pertaining to Myerhoff's study.

1. Which type of research method did Myerhoff use in her study of elderly Jews in Venice, California?

   a. survey
   b. field
   c. experiment
   d. content analysis

2. Which method of sociological research does anthropological research most closely resemble?

   a. survey
   b. field
   c. experiment
   d. content analysis

3. Specifically which approach did Myerhoff use in her study?

   a. participant-observation, known to sample
   b. participant-observation, unknown to sample
   c. non-participant observation, known to sample
   d. non-participant observation, unknown to sample

4. What methodological function(s) did the Living History classes serve for Myerhoff?

   a. collect data
   b. select sample
   c. provide skills to the seniors
   d. a and c only
   e. all of the above

5. Which of the following was of major concern to Myerhoff when she began her research?

   a. bias
   b. researching human subjects
   c. common sense

6. What was one technique employed by Myerhoff to get a better understanding of her sample?

7. Name one other methodological tool that you think Myerhoff could have used in her study.

   Why did you select this particular tool? What do you think are its advantages?

Chapter 9

Tools and Data:
First Day on the Job

The high turnover rates among young employees has been a major concern of employers, educators, policymakers, scholars, and young adults themselves. The National Institute of Education has funded research to determine the factors that influence the resignations and firings of young people. One of these studies focused on the processes involved in gaining and maintaining employment, as well as losing or changing employment (Borman, et al., 1984). It included a field study directed by co-author Jane Reisman, who used observational and interview data based on the lives of 24 youths in two midwestern cities.

The following is an excerpt from Reisman's field notes on a young female office worker's first day on a new job. While in high school, this employee had worked part-time for the same company as an intern. Shortly after graduation, she began full-time employment in a different department. Read the field notes and respond to the assessment questions that follow.

Identifiers:

Date: 6/13/83
Place: Insurance company (IC)
Background: First day on the job
Participants: Val (new hire), M (manager), co-workers (mainly Sue, Julie, and Barb), and observer [comments in brackets].

8:00 A.M.

Val begins the day by meeting with her new boss M (Director of Agency Administration). They meet in his office. He sits behind his large, uncluttered wooden desk. She sits across from him [as I did].

M wants to explain IC's distribution system and "how we sell insurance." He informs her that insurance agents are contractual agents—not employees. "Important distinction. Keep that in the back of your mind." M continues to explain the licensing process. [He is using sophisticated language but occasionally uses football analogies such as "the whole nine yards."]

"At this point, I don't want to fill your head with a lot of details that don't mean a whole lot to you. . . . I want to give you work stuff. Hopefully, it will make more sense to you later."

Still, he continues to explain.

There are distinctions between agents, brokers, and part-time agents. "We handle all administration. We are like the personnel department, computer department, finance. . . as it relates to the field. We are here as a service organizations to the field. That's our primary function.

"As time goes on, you are going to get to know the agents. You may start to feel that someone is a real jerk. But keep in mind, we are here to serve the agents. If they are not there selling insurance, we would not be here either. We will do our best to accommodate the field, but we can't violate the rules."

M reviews the scope of work in the office. . . . As far as this week goes, Val will be expected to distribute the pension plans, a 3-4 hour task, and begin working on terminations. "There are certain things we have to do with those contracts. There is a rush to get someone loaded in the system. Otherwise, they don't get paid. It's not the case with termination. There's a stack out there. We have to get those caught up. You are going to be doing that all the time. . . ."

M calls co-worker Sue on phone. Asks her to come to his office. Meanwhile, he asks Val, "What do people call you?"

Val: "Val."

M: "Everyone calls me M. We can call you VW."

Val: "No, Val."

M: "Valerie?"

Val: "Val."

[Val is wearing a pink cotton shirt with the collars fashionably folded upward, purple and pink flax slacks, and flat white shoes. Her dress is casual. Her hair is shoulder-length, blonde and wavy, fashionably styled—angled off her face, short in the front and longer in the back. She is chewing gum during the morning meeting—in fact, throughout most of the day.]

M reads a letter to Val. Sue arrives. M points to a stack of computer printouts. Asks Sue if they (printout names) are full-time only. Affirmative.

"Val, I am going to give you an opportunity to be creative right off the bat. I want you to recompose this letter. One, I want you to change the dates. Two, I want you to put in a sentence like—" M writes and mumbles aloud. He hands her the letter across the desk.

Now, a second letter. M revises it while Val and Sue attentively sit, watching him.

"So, redo these two letters." M pulls printout stack over to him, examines it and questions Sue about the accuracy of some information. Hands stack to her. "Then this afternoon, we'll work on termination procedures. "Why don't we get started? Sue will be the one to answer any questions you may have. (Looking at Sue) Could you maybe take Val around the floor and introduce her to everyone?"

Sue: "O.K."

[The training session lasted 45 minutes. Sue and Val return to the clerical area. There are five other office workers in this division. Sue and another woman appear to be the youngest—late 20's/early 30's. They are both fashionably dressed and trim. The other three women are noticeably overweight and also less groomed or fashionable. They appear to range in age between mid 30's and and mid 50's. Val is 18.

Each office worker has her own desk, adding machine with video display unit and typewriter. Julie also has a microfiche on her desk. Another microfiche sits on the table in the rear of the office. The walls are bare save for a picture of a lake and a wall clock (on the private office wall). The room has file cabinets on its eastern border. Stacks of paper and a couple of scraggly philodendra cuttings set on top of the cabinets.]

M approaches Julie. She shows him pictures of her baby granddaughter. He responds knowingly and with seeming interest.

Val returns from her introductory tour and goes to her desk. Begins reading letter and commences to revise it. Lights a cigarette. Inserts letter into typewriter and types it.

Julie: "Hi, I am Julie."

Val: "Hi."

Val shows letter to woman behind her (Barb) and asks for help identifying a written word.

Barb: "He (M) has a reputation for being a lousy writer."

Val: "Just like Carl (former boss)."

A new woman enters the office area.

Barb: "Val, this is Mary. You may have seen her down on five (fifth floor). She came to visit me."

Two of the office workers chat with Mary.

M enters the room. Sees Val smoking.

M: "I finally hired someone who smokes. Someone else to bum cigarettes from."

He exits.

Laurie: "He will, too, he's a bummer."

Sue returns. Asks Val if she found some of M's stationary.

Val: "Yes, it was in my drawer."

Sue explains material to her. Val and Sue continue working while others chat with each other.

9:00

Val continues typing. When finished, she compares newly typed letter with draft. She exits to M's office.

Her phone rings. Sue answers it for her and takes a message. Val returns to her desk and dials phone, hangs up. She exits again for a break. [Break lasts 20 minutes.]

While Val is gone, the others work and talk. A man walks into the office and talks about his wife, the heat, and women's lib. He leaves after a few minutes.

One co-worker asks Sue, "Does Val have everything she needs?"

Sue: "I think so, I went through her desk quickly this morning. Gave her some calculator tape."

Another asks: "Does Val smoke?"

Sue: "I don't know."

Another: "Well, I see an ash tray with a cigarette on her desk."

Val returns. M comes over to her desk and looks at her work. He comments about her task and leaves. Val asks Sue for a certain form. Tells Sue that she is going over to the print shop. Sue hands her a form and tells her a code number.

9:55

Val exits. Returns after five minutes. Begins to examine stack of printouts. Sue walks over to her desk. Shows her a form and begins to talk about it.

Sue begins to update the printouts based on information from the index files. Sue tells Val she needs a certain type of envelope and calls someone on the telephone to have the envelopes sent over.

Sue returns to her desk. Val thumbs through the printouts. She refolds some sheets and tears them apart into smaller groups. She smokes another cigarette while she works. (She works quietly, methodically, and without any apparent hurry.)

11:00

Still separating printout files. She completes this separating task at 11:10 and begins thumbing through the index files.

Sue approaches Val's desk and gives her new information.

Val: "O.K."

Val's phone rings.

Val: "Agency, Val speaking." Silence.

"Hi." Laughs. "Let's see. Sue, what time does everyone go to lunch?"

Sue: "You can go at 11:30 if you want."

Val: "11:30, I'll meet you there."

Val returns to looking through filing cards, while Sue reviews what time everyone goes to lunch.

11:30

Val leaves for lunch.

EXERCISE
for *Tools and Data,* Chapter 9

Name_____Date_____

Assessment questions 1-3 concern the content and structure of the field notes themselves; questions 4-7 pertain to analyzing the notes. The reliability of field data as "hard data" depends strongly on whether several different analysts who interpret the notes reach similar conclusions.

1. Provide a hypothetical expansion of Reisman's field notes for the period between 9:55 and 11:00 A.M. to include further details, such as co-workers' activities, facial expressions, actual telephone conversations, and so on.

2. Two behaviors recorded in the field notes are gum chewing and cigarette smoking. Considering that the information recorded in the notes should be relevant to Val's potential for maintaining employment, do you believe that these behaviors should be included? Explain.

3. List two limitations of the observer's role in terms of recording field notes.

(1)

(2)

4. List three social interactions or comments which might help Val feel comfortable in her new job.

(1)

(2)

(3)

5. Describe Val's approach to her new job.

6. Which of the following members of the workplace had a part in Val's socialization to her new job during the first morning of work?

    a. Boss
    b. Co-workers
    c. Personnel department
    d. a and b
    e. All of the above

7. Which of the following best describes the mood of Val's office environment during the observation period?

    a. Stoic
    b. Friendly
    c. Formal
    d. Intimidating

Chapter 9

Application:
Field Research

Imagine that you have joined a large-scale investigation of how power and control develop in social interactions. Your responsibility is to be either an observer or a participant-observer in one of the following settings:

- workplace
- classroom
- playground
- team practice
- organization meeting
- restaurant

The project director asks you to proceed as follows:

1. Choose one of the actual settings as listed above, and act as either an observer or a participant-observer for one to three hours.

2. Record your prior knowledge of the "scene," including biases and preconceived notions based on your own views and what you have read.

3. Take notes of your observations, including as many quotes as possible. (If you cannot take complete notes during the observation itself, jot down key words and flesh out the details afterwards.)

4. In addition to recording your observations, make note of your reactions to what you have observed. These notes may be recorded separately or integrated with the observation notes. If your reactions are integrated with the notes, be sure to distinguish them by using brackets, capital letters, writing them in the margins, or any other method of your choosing.

5. Review your notes at a later time (the same day or another day) and develop tentative conclusions based on them.

6. Submit a report that includes your prior knowledge of the scene, your observational notes and reactions, and your tentative conclusions. The report should be between five and ten pages in length.

Name_____Date_____

REPORT

Prior Knowledge of the Scene:

Observation Notes: (Attach to this report.)

Your Reactions: (Provide reactions in this space if they are not integrated with the observation notes.)

Tentative Conclusions:

Chapter 10

'Wanted: Subjects for Experimental Study': Experiments and Quasi-Experiments

✓ *Research Brief:*

'L.A. Law'—Stay Tuned for the Next Episode

✓ *Tools and Data:*

Assigning Blame for Rape

✓ *Application:*

Experimental and Comparison Groups

Chapter 10

Research Brief:

'L.A. Law'—Stay Tuned for the Next Episode

How much influence should an experiment have on a judge's or jury's decision in an obscenity trial? According to Daniel Linz and his research team (1991), experimental data are crucial to the prosecution because they help to define a "community standard" to determine whether or not communicative material (films, books, magazines, etc.) is pornographic. Any other means of arriving at a community standard, typically based on a judge's or jurors' impressions of what their community can tolerate, becomes simply guesswork. Research by Linz and his colleagues showed that such guesswork may significantly underestimate a community's level of tolerance, since people generally assume that their neighbors are less tolerant than they actually are. In contrast, the experimental procedures developed by Linz's group offer an empirically-based method for estimating community standards, which can be used as expert testimony in obscenity prosecutions.

One experiment conducted by Linz's group was designed for use in a 1989 case, *The State of North Carolina v. Cinema Blue of Charlotte, Inc.* The purpose of the study was to "gather social science data to inform the jury as to whether the average adult in Mecklenburg County, North Carolina, applying contemporary community standards, would find that five movies and one magazine alleged to be obscene by the state either appealed to a prurient interest in sex or were patently offensive" (p. 86).

In designing their study, the researchers considered the decision by North Carolina's Supreme Court that such data could be used as expert witness testimony in obscenity prosecutions as long as the study was *"conducted pursuant to accepted methodology, and the opinions garnered therefrom were relevant to the issues before the court"* (p. 85; emphasis added). At that time, only public opinion survey research had been used in obscenity cases. Although the "accepted methodology" contingency was not a problem with public opinion survey research, certain results were excluded because they did not specifically focus on the type of materials involved in the case, or because the survey's language was deemed too vague and inadequate to convey the visual impact of the material under prosecution.

The researchers determined that their experimental approach should meet the following criteria: (1) the use of conventional social scientific research standards, (2) direct relevance to the materials contested in the case, and (3) the communication of visual impact equivalent to that of the contested materials. Below are the procedures they used to meet these criteria:

Sampling. A random sample of adult residents of Mecklenburg County, North Carolina, were contacted by telephone and invited to participate in the study. Those who agreed to participate were randomly assigned to either test (experimental) or control conditions. (One hundred and ten subjects were assigned to test conditions, nineteen subjects to control conditions.) The subjects did not know whether they were assigned to test or control conditions until they reported to their viewing sessions.

Conditions. Test conditions involved viewing one of five sexually explicit, X-rated films alleged to be obscene at the commencement of the study. (Charges against three of the films were subsequently dropped.) A subsample of subjects assigned to one of the X-rated film groups also read an allegedly obscene magazine. Control conditions involved viewing a non-explicit film.

Measures. Prefilm (pretest) and postfilm (posttest) questionnaires were administered, as well as a postmagazine (posttest) questionnaire for subjects assigned to the film and magazine group.

The prefilm questionnaire included background questions, such as the length of one's residence in Mecklenburg County, religious persuasion, and rate of video movie consumption. Three questions related to obscenity attitudes: (1) one's perception of the community's tolerance of adult movies, video cassettes, and magazines showing nudity and sex; (2) one's belief in the individual's right to view sex acts in adult movies, video cassettes, or magazines; and (3) one's belief that showing sex acts in great detail with closeups of sexual organs appeals to an unhealthy, morbid, or prurient interest in sex.

The postfilm and postmagazine questionnaires included questions regarding a number of contemporary issues, such as gun control, censorship, and religious tolerance, as well as a repetition of the prefilm questions on obscenity attitudes. The subjects were also asked whether the movie or magazine was what they expected to see, given the definition of "X-rated" provided in the prefilm questionnaire, and whether they had ever previously seen a film or video like the one they just viewed and, if so, how many times in the last five years.

Analysis.   The researchers compared pretest and posttest responses to the obscenity attitude questions, as well as test and control groups to detect a testing effect.   Analyses of the representativeness of the sample were also performed to detect potential sampling bias.

The results of this experiment revealed that the subjects did not feel that the films or magazine appealed to a prurient interest in sex or exceeded the level of tolerance of the average resident of Mecklenburg County.   Interestingly enough, the study participants reported greater personal tolerance of these materials than, in their opinion, the "average person" in their county.   Another curious finding was that participants' pretest responses to the question of whether these films appealed to a prurient interest changed significantly on the posttest.   After viewing the material first-hand, they were far less likely to consider it as appealing to a prurient interest in sex.

Statistical tests to determine the sample's representativeness indicated a potential selection bias in at least two categories: more male than female volunteers and more middle-aged (30-49) volunteers than volunteers from younger (18-29) or older (50+) age categories.   Statistical corrections of the responses, in order to detect the effects of this potential selection bias, suggest that it did not affect the survey results.

ASSESSMENT QUESTIONS
for *Research Brief,* Chapter 10

Name_____Date_____

Answer the following questions pertaining to the preceding research brief.

1. What advantage does an experiment have over a survey in addressing the court's concern about visual impact?

    a. The experimental conditions can provide a visual experience that is the same or similar to the one relevant to the trial.
    b. The experimental conditions can include both pretest and posttest measurements.
    c. An experimental design can include both a test group and a control group.
    d. No advantage is obvious.

2. For an obscenity prosecution, which of the following are the potential disadvantages of Linz's et al. experimental method compared to the use of a public opinion survey?

    a. More time-consuming for study participants
    b. More time-consuming for overall administration of the study
    c. More costly
    d. All of the above
    e. None of the above

3. Discuss how common sense may have affected the accuracy of estimating the "average person's" tolerance for allegedly obscene material?

4. What was the potential effect of bias in this experiment?

How did the researchers control this potential problem?

5. What is your reaction to the researchers' claim that social science experiments have an important place in obscenity prosecutions?

Chapter 10

Tools and Data:
Assigning Blame for Rape

Do we blame victims for their misfortune? According to Shaver's (1970) "defensive attribution" concept, we are more likely to blame those victims who are different from ourselves than those who are similar. In this way, we protect ourselves from blame in the event that we ourselves become the victim.

Lisa Lubomski and her colleagues (1987) designed an experiment to test the applicability of this concept to rape victims, both male and female. The researchers hypothesized that "subjects would attribute the least responsibility for the rape to victims who were most similar to them, both in terms of sex and in terms of age and status" (1987, p. 1).

Eighty female and eighty male students at a private liberal arts college participated in the experiment. The design used brief descriptions of sexual assault crimes in the form of summaries from actual police reports. The descriptions of the victims in the reports varied by sex—female or male—and age, combined with status (e.g., a 21-year-old college student or a 45-year-old, unemployed, recovering alcoholic).

The following is a sample of a summary used in this experiment:

DEPARTMENTAL CORRESPONDENCE

DATE :   7/30/86
SUBJECT: #7894-KD of 7/29/86
TO: JKL, Chief Clerk   DEPT: Records
FROM: VQS Investigating Officer DEPT: Felony

While walking to the bus stop at 10th and Commerce, the victim, Jane W., was accosted by the defendant, Charles E. A struggle took place between the two, in which Jane W. was raped by Charles E. A passerby heard the victim calling for help and telephoned this department, where the call was received at 9:00 p.m. Officers Sims and Hall arrived approximately 10 minutes later, and apprehended the defendant, who was positively identified by Jane W.

Description of the defendant: Charles E.

Charles E. is a muscular male, 5'10" in height, 175 pounds, 31 years of age. He is employed as an auto mechanic at a local service station.

Description of the victim: Jane W.

Jane W. is 5'6", 130 pounds, 21 years of age. She is a college student, attending classes at a local college.

Some sample questions follow:

Blame Measure:

How likely is it that the victim did something to encourage the incident?

_____Not at all likely   _____Somewhat likely
_____Moderately likely   _____Highly likely

How likely do you think it is that the victim being victimized was due to chance?

_____Not at all likely   _____Somewhat likely
_____Moderately likely   _____Highly likely

Similarity Measure

How similar do you feel the victim is to you?-

_____Not at all similar   _____Somewhat similar
_____Moderately similar   _____Highly similar

Probability Measure

How respectable do you think the victim is?

_____Not at all respectable   _____Somewhat respectable
_____Moderately respectable   _____Highly respectable

The summaries were then randomly assigned to the participating students, who were asked to respond to questions concerning the extent of the victim's responsibility, such as whether the victim provoked or encouraged the assault, was careless, and/or could have prevented the assault. Questions about the victim's likeability, respectability, and similarity to the subject were also included.

Responses to the questions were scored from one ("Not at all") to seven ("Highly"). The data were analyzed using the "analysis of variance" statistic (ANOVA). Results of some of these ANOVA tests are provided in Table 1.

Table 1. Effects of Subject Sex and Victim Similarity on Attributions of Blame of, Similarity to, and Respectability of the Victim

		Independent Variables				
		Subject Sex			Victim Similarity	
		Category Means			Category Means	
Dependent Variables	F	Male	Female	F	Male	Female
Victim Encouraged	4.24*	2.53	2.13	4.24*	2.13	2.53
Victim By Chance	3.98*	4.28	4.89	0.12*	4.59	4.68
Victim Similarity	4.38*	2.63	3.09	61.83***	3.72	1.99
Victim Respectability	1.06	4.44	4.66	31.51***	5.16	3.94

* $p < .05$
** $p < .01$
*** $p < .001$

Note that the F ratio provides a statistical test for comparing the sample means. These ratios are given "significance levels" based on how they fit on a mathematical distribution referred to as the F distribution. Significance levels of .05 or less are conventionally regarded as "statistically significant." In other words, a significance level of .05 suggests that the study groups are significantly different from each other and that their differences are not due simply to chance. Significance levels are often denoted as "p" for probability.

Given such an interpretive framework, the statistical results provided in Table 1 lend mixed support to the researchers' hypotheses. Turn to the assessment questions for help in interpreting these results.

ASSESSMENT QUESTIONS
for *Tools and Data*, Chapter 10

Name_____Date_____

1. Circle the level of statistical significance for each of the following relationships. (Refer to Table 1 in providing your answers.)

Victim Encouraged and Subject Sex	p>.05	p<.05	p<.01	p<.001
Victim by Chance and Subject Sex	p>.05	p<.05	p<.01	p<.001
Victim by Chance and Victim Similarity	p>.05	p<.05	p<.01	p<.001
Victim Respectability and Subject Sex	p>.05	p<.05	p<.01	p<.001

2. Consider the relationship between victim similarity and subject sex. Which sex is significantly more likely to regard itself as similar to the victim?

    Male   _____

    Female   _____

3. Consider the two dependent variables which are Blame Measures: victim by chance and victim encouraged. Which of these measures is significantly affected by the independent variable of victim similarity?

    a. Victim encouraged
    b. Victim by chance
    c. Both
    d. Neither

4. Which results provide support for the research hypothesis that "subjects would attribute the least responsibility for the rape to victims who were most similar to themselves in terms of sex and in terms of age and status"?

Which results disconfirm this hypothesis?

5. Risk to human subjects is an important concern when studying a sensitive subject such as rape. List two precautionary measures that the researchers might have taken to protect the participants in this experiment.

1)

2)

Chapter **10**

 Application:

Experimental and Comparison Groups

*Name*_____*Date*_____

The key to experimental design is the introduction of an independent variable to the experimental group but not to the control group. This enables the researchers to test for any change in the dependent variable on the part of the experimental group resulting from the treatment or intervention of the independent variable.

This application focuses on one concern of experiments and quasi-experiments, the assignment of individuals to the experimental and control groups. While the classic experimental design utilizes the random assignment of subjects to groups, quasi-experimental design can differ in how group assignments are made. For example, matching may be used to produce two groups that are as similar as possible in all variables prior to the introduction of the independent variable. This approach pairs individuals with similar characteristics, then assigns one member of the pair to the experimental group and the other to the comparison group; e.g., a female to the experimental group and a female to the comparison group, an Hispanic and a medical student to each group. The characteristics used as a basis for matching are determined by the nature of the study.

Procedure:

1. Select a topic or question for study that is appropriate for quasi-experimental design.
2. Identify the dependent and independent variables.
3. Determine the treatment or intervention to be introduced to the experimental group as the independent variable.
4. Determine the time frame for conducting the pretest, introducing the treatment or intervention, and for conducting the posttest.
5. Determine the nature of the experimental group and the comparison group. Describe what you want your two groups to be like and specify how you would go about recruiting subjects and assigning them to each group.

Write-up:

1. Topic/question:

2. Variables:
   Dependent:

   Independent:

3. Experimental Group Treatment/Intervention:

4. Time Frame:
   Pretest:

   Intervention:

   Posttest:

5. Group Selection – Experimental Group
   Description:

   Number:

Social Characteristics:

a.

b.

c.

d.

e.

Selection Procedure:

Group Selection – Comparison Group
Description:

Number:

Social Characteristics:

a.

b.

c.

d.

e.

Selection Procedure:

Chapter 11

Thumbs Up or Down? Evaluation and Applied Research

✔ *Research Brief:*

'And One More Thing . . .'

✔ *Tools and Data:*

Can the Racial Attitudes of Elementary School Students be Changed?

✔ *Application:*

Measuring Program Effectiveness

Chapter 11

Research Brief:
'And One More Thing . . .'

Imagine this scenario. A patient in New York State, who has just undergone successful hip surgery, is upset because the surgeon did not operate on her ailing elbow at the same time. The patient complains that, since her elbow is still painful, the surgeon did not do her job properly. She asks the doctor to perform additional surgery on her elbow—gratis. The surgeon replies that she would be glad to perform the surgery, if warranted, but at the usual fee.

Most of us would not be surprised by the surgeon's response. We in the United States are well accustomed to the fee-per-service system of medicine, which charges separately for each medical procedure, including exams, consultations, and surgery.

This mutual understanding has not evolved in the same way between sociologists and their clients, according to sociologist Craig Little. In an article about applied research practice, Little describes a situation in which one of his clients expected him to supply additional data analyses and reports beyond what was originally contracted for, but without further pay—as if they were rightfully due the client. Little refused to do so, even at the risk of his reputation.

In 1977, Little was approached by members of a youth services board in Cortland, New York. Apparently, the State required that counties conduct systematic and comprehensive "needs assessments" in order to be eligible for youth services funding. The board asked Little to conduct a survey of the county's young people in order to fulfill this requirement.

Little provided sociological expertise in the design and development of the survey project, which utilized a 97-item questionnaire. Respondents were asked to rate the frequency and seriousness of a wide range of problems affecting young people, and to indicate their own personal needs and the needs of youth in general. The county took responsibility for many of the labor-intensive tasks, such as data coding and data entry, as a cost-saving measure. Little was responsible for analyzing the data and providing a final report, in the form of a descriptive analysis of the survey data, for the Cortland Youth Bureau. Such an analysis typically reports percentages for each of the survey items.

Little completed the project as planned and presented the findings at a meeting with the Youth Bureau. During the meeting, he agreed to write a supplemental memo comparing the survey's findings on delinquency with other survey results described in criminological research literature. Little regarded this supplemental information as a bonus to the County, since it was not called for in their contractual agreement.

Several months later, the director of the Youth Bureau requested that Little provide further analyses of the data pertaining to possible differences in responses based either on gender or school districts, even though this exceeded the requirements of a univariate data analysis. Willing, nevertheless, to perform these analyses, Little informed the director that he would get back to him shortly with an estimate of his fee. When the director consulted with his legislative committee to obtain funding for the additional analyses, he was told that the Youth Bureau should already have all the information it needed from the original report. If additional information were required, it was the responsibility of the *researcher* to provide it.

Little felt that this expectation was unfair and unprofessional. With a survey of almost 100 items, the possibilities for analysis were virtually limitless. In the absence of clearly defined norms, such as those that govern doctor-patient relationships, there could have been an unending stream of demands for further service without compensation. Politely but firmly, Little declined to supply anything further. Fortunately, he was successful in communicating his viewpoint. The Youth Bureau subsequently contracted with him to conduct similar surveys in 1983 and 1989, during which Little detailed precisely the type of services he would provide. This included a well-defined final "product," such as a report, that represented the end of his contractual obligations.

ASSESSMENT QUESTIONS
for *Research Brief,* Chapter 11

Name_____Date_____

Answer the following questions pertaining to the preceding research brief.

1. Which of the following best describes the purpose of Little's research?

    a. To measure the level of juvenile delinquency in Cortland, New York.
    b. To compare the needs of youth in New York State with youth in other states.
    c. To provide Professor Little with a large data base for conducting further research.
    d. To assess a wide range of youth problems and needs as required by a state government funding source.

2. Which of the following descriptions best characterizes Little's view of a fee-per-service arrangement in research?

    a. The client pays the researcher a fee based upon specific services detailed in advance.
    b. The researcher and client reach an agreement about which services will be charged for and which will be donated.
    c. The client determines the amount of payment to the researcher according to how satisfied he/she is with the final product.
    d. The researcher is paid more if the findings are favorable to the client.

3. Discuss the potential influence of bias when the researcher is paid directly by the client.

4. To what extent do you consider the comparison between the doctor-patient relationship and the researcher-client relationship to be valid? Discuss.

5. Imagine yourself in Little's situation when the director asked him to supply additional analyses and reports. How would you have responded?

Chapter 11

Tools and Data:

Can the Racial Attitudes of Elementary School Students Be Changed?

Anne Hendershott and three colleagues (1991) at the University of Hartford evaluated a Connecticut program intended to reduce racial prejudice and discrimination. This "cooperative learning" program—one of 27 interdistrict projects throughout the state to reduce the effects of racial segregation—brought together students from different racial groups. The evaluation focused on the effects of this short-term experience on children's attitudes toward teachers and other children of a different race.

Two schools were involved in the program, each of which was relatively segregated— one 75 percent black and the other 88 percent white. For a period of eight weeks, children in grades one through four met for a full day each week to discuss the themes of Community, Communication, Environment and Working Together. Teachers and program staff participated in a training seminar prior to the beginning of the program.

The research investigated the question of "whether cooperative experience generated any detectable changes in students' attitudes toward those of a different race or had any effect on the social distance between those of a different race." The researchers adapted pretest and posttest measures for use with the sample group, as well as randomly selected control groups, comprised of 165 program students and 152 control students. Data analyses included data from students of the racial majority at each school—111 program students (63 white and 48 black) and 78 control students (40 white and 38 black).

The tools to be used included three attitudinal measures which were group-administered, i.e., answered in class at designated time periods:

1. Social Distance. Each student was given a booklet containing five color pictures of a group of white students, a group of black students, an integrated group of students, a black teacher, and a white teacher. Also included was a race- and sex-appropriate set of pregummed, paper doll-like "self figures"—either black or white, female or male. Students were instructed to "paste themselves" wherever they wanted to be in the pictures featuring the black, white, and integrated students. The social distance measure was scored by calculating the distance between the center of the self figure to the center of the target figure, to the nearest centimeter. This measure was adapted from a social distance measure designed by Koslin, Amarel, and Ames (1968).

2. **Interest in Joining Diverse Groups.** Students were shown pictures of groups of children in three settings—home, playground, and classroom. The racial composition of the groups varied from all black to integrated to all white. Students were asked of each picture if they wanted to be part of that group, then instructed to indicate their answer by coloring in *yes, no,* or *do not know*. This measure was adapted from one designed by Koslin, Koslin, and Pargament (1972).

3. **Desirability of Story Characters.** Two short stories were read to female children, each featuring a white and black female character respectively, and to male children, each with a white and black male character. Students heard the same stories during the pretest and posttest phases of the project. They were then asked three questions pertaining to whether they would like to play with, be a friend of, and invite home the central character in each story. This measure was created especially for this study.

Differences between the experimental and the control groups were analyzed for changes in mean scores on the pretests and posttests in order to determine the degree to which racial attitudes may have changed as a result of participation in the program.

Research on racial attitudes among young children can be challenging. While racial attitudes appear to be well-developed by age three, they have not yet crystallized and are still developing during grade school years (Katz, 1976). As Newman, Liss, and Sherman (1983) cautioned, "children's ethnic awareness and attitudes are not only highly complex, but may also be a function of stimulus material, question format, and locale." So validity tests were conducted prior to the analysis to determine whether the children were capable of distinguishing the race of pictured individuals and whether they tended to make same-race preferences.

For the Social Distance measure, it was assumed by the researchers based on literature in the field that pretested white students would indicate greater distances from the pictured black teacher than from the pictured white teacher, from all-black peers than from integrated peers, and the least distance from white peers. Conversely, it was expected that this predicted rank order would show the reverse for pretested black students. The validity check indicated that 69 percent of the rank comparisons were in the presumed order. Therefore, the researchers felt relatively confident that the social distance measure was a valid indicator of racial attitude, and that differences between pretest and posttest scores would reflect predicted changes in racial attitudes.

For the Interest in Joining Diverse Groups measure, the researchers expected that black children would be most interested in joining black peers, less interested in joining an integrated group, and least interested in joining white peers, and that the reverse trend would be true for white students. A comparison of pretest rankings of both groups served as a validity check, with 75 percent corresponding to the predicted order. This also contributed to the researchers' confidence that changes in pretest and posttest rankings would indicate the same changes in racial attitudes.

Observations made by the researchers during the posttest phase served as a reliability check. Attitudes of boredom were exhibited by some of the students when they had to complete the same exercises a second time, especially the Desirability of Story Characters measure. Not only had the children already heard the stories before, but since they were just being asked to respond *yes, no,* or *do not know* to questions about the story, they were not as actively involved as they had been during the pretest phase. As a result, the researchers questioned the reliability of this measure.

The results of the study were mixed. The only statistically significant results were produced by the Social Distance measure, and only on the part of black students who indicated less social distance from integrated settings, white students, and white teachers than white students from integrated settings, black students, and black teachers. No significant results were achieved from the other two measures.

The researchers concluded that, although the cooperative program showed mixed results, it did demonstrate some effectiveness in reducing racial segregation and, to some degree, racial prejudice. Very obvious to the researchers, apparently, was the challenge of ensuring that the instruments used in assessing the attitudes of young children were valid and reliable.

ASSESSMENT QUESTIONS
for *Tools and Data,* Chapter 11

Name_____Date_____

Answer the following questions pertaining to the study conducted by Hendershott et al.

1. What type of validity did the researchers check for in the pretests?

    a. criterion-related
    b. content
    c. construct
    d. face validity

2. What was one potential problem with establishing the reliability of the tools used in this evaluation study?

3. What was one potential problem with establishing the validity of the measures used in this evaluation study?

4. What was one important reason associated with validity for using pretests as well as posttests in this evaluation study?

    a. To determine if there had been any changes in attitudes.
    b. To determine if children understood the concept of race at the time of the posttest.
    c. To determine if the measure used was appropriate for determining the existence of racial attitude.
    d. To determine if the measure would yield the same results with each test.

5. Describe another approach to establishing validity for any one of the three measures in this study. Name the measure and specify what could be done with the children to check the accuracy of the measure as an indicator.

6. Describe another approach to establishing reliability for any one of the three measures in this study. Name the measure and specify what could be done with the children to check for the consistency of the measure as an indicator.

Chapter 11

Application:
Measuring Program Effectiveness

*Name*_____*Date*_____

Select a social or educational program which interests you, such as a Head Start, Rape Relief, Big Brother/Big Sister, or study-abroad program. List three to five measurements to assess the program's level of success, e.g., 60 percent or greater program completion, client satisfaction, and community support.

List of Measurements:

1.

2.

3.

4.

5.

Arrange individual interviews (by telephone or face-to-face) with the program director and a staff person of your selected program. Cover the following points in both interviews:

(1) Describe the goals of the program.
(2) Discuss the appropriateness of the success measures you identified.
(3) Suggest additional measures that could have successful results.

Evaluate the interview responses and prepare a report analyzing the issues outlined on the next page.

REPORT

Program Name_____

Address_____

Telephone Number(s)_____

Director's Name_____

Staff Member's Name and Responsibility_____

_____

Program Goals

Director's View of Program's Goals:

Staff Member's View of Program's Goals:

Reaction to Your Success Measures

Director's Reaction:

Staff Member's Reaction:

Suggestions for Additional Measures

Director's Suggestions:

Staff Member's Suggestions:

As a researcher, in what way, if any, would you change the success measures which you initially identified? (This question requires an analysis of the preceding information.) Explain your decision based on the interview responses.

Plans for Modifications of your Success Measures:

Explanation:

Chapter 12

No-Contact Research: Unobtrusive Methods

✓ *Research Brief:*

Where Are Women and Minorities in the Computer Revolution?

✓ *Tools and Data:*

Using Historical Records to Expose the Myth of the Absent Family

✓ *Application:*

Content Analysis Project

Chapter 12

Research Brief:
Where Are Women and Minorities in the Computer Revolution?

A content analysis study of computer magazines and journals revealed the disturbing finding that ". . .white men are the masters of computers but women and minorities are onlookers" (Demetrulias and Rosenthal, 1985, p. 95). This study was performed by two professors of education, Diana Mayer Demetrulias and Nina Ribak Rosenthal, in order to assess gender and racial stereotypes in computer advertising. The researchers proposed that biased advertising may have an adverse affect on educators' attempts to attract women and minorities to careers in computer fields.

Numerous studies conducted in the 1980s revealed computer-related equity problems—inequality in computer-use patterns in secondary schools, in programming class enrollments in both elementary and secondary schools, and in attendance at computer camps. Research on advertising, in general, concluded that women were frequently depicted as decorative ornaments, and textbook illustrations were found to convey racial stereotypes. Therefore, Demetrulias and Rosenthal believed that gender and racial stereotyping in visual advertising would reflect cultural stereotyping in the use of computers.

Their research design used content analysis to measure sexism and racism both quantitatively and qualitatively. The quantitative measurement employed a frequency count by gender and race. Qualitative measurement included descriptions of the relationships among people in advertisements, the type of setting, the use of computers, and additional descriptive features or comments. Recording tools were developed and validated, and coders were trained. As a result, intercoder reliability reached an appropriate level of 85 percent. (In other words, coders agreed with each other 85 percent of the time.)

All the issues of 15 journals and magazines published between August, 1982, and January, 1984, including *BYTE, Computerworld, Mathematics Teacher,* and

Popular Computing, were selected for analysis. This amounted to 172 publications with a total of 1,139 advertisements related to computers. However, the final sample was reduced to 167 advertisements when duplicate advertisements and those that did not display people were eliminated from the sampling frame.

Analysis procedures included statistical examination and qualitative analysis, which could reveal latent patterns. Statistical procedures used comparisons between the people depicted in the advertisements and the percent distribution of people by gender and race according to the 1980 census. Chi square tests, with Yates corrections, were performed on these distributions.

The research results revealed a substantial amount of gender and racial stereotyping. Statistical analyses showed significant over-representation of white males, both men and boys. For example, 61 percent of the children in the advertisements were boys, although boys made up only 51 percent of the child population in the 1980 census. Similarly, men who comprise only 49 percent of the adult population appeared in the ads 75 percent of the time.

Race was more difficult to analyze than gender, because most pictures did not provide enough detail to clearly identify people by race. For this portion of the analysis the valid number of advertisements was reduced to 26 entries, which included 186 children and 317 adults. In these ads non-whites were displayed significantly less often than might be expected, based on the census data.

The qualitative analyses revealed further evidence of gender and racial stereotyping. For example, the most common type of advertisement (59 percent) featured a "lone adult male" (p. 93), usually a famous actor or historical figure, such as William Shatner or Benjamin Franklin. In 90 percent of these ads the males were white. In fact, only one non-white male was ever shown—Bill Cosby. Women were shown as a lone adult figure in only eight ads. In these cases, the women were white, feminine in appearance, and presented in a stereotypical female setting, such as the home or kitchen.

Feminine imagery and roles pervaded all of the advertisements featuring women or girls. Women kept flowers and purses on their computer tables. In one ad, girls displayed records, hair ribbons, and hairbrushes. Women and girls were always shown smiling and were usually located peripherally—either standing beside or looking down at the top of the computer monitor. In contrast, the men and boys were shown *working* at the computer, their facial expressions conveying either satisfaction or frustration.

From these and other findings, the researchers concluded that advertisements in computer journals and magazines portray males, females, whites, and racial/ethnic minorities differently. They contended that such discrepancies perpetuate the gender and racial stereotypes underlying computer inequities. They dismiss the argument that advertisers are simply reflecting prevailing social values—showing what is rather than what ought to be. Instead, they advance the theory that such advertisements are shaping social reality itself—by portraying the computer field as a white male-dominated world.

ASSESSMENT QUESTIONS
for *Research Brief,* Chapter 12

Name_____Date_____

Answer the following questions pertaining to the preceding research brief.

1. Which of the following conclusions can be reached on the basis of Demutrulias' and Rosenthal's research?

    a. Males are more proficient at computer technology than are females.
    b. Females have less opportunity to learn computing than do males.
    c. Computer advertisements attempt to appeal to members of racial/ethnic minorities.
    d. Computer advertisements perpetuate gender and racial stereotypes related to computing.
    e. All of the above.

2. Which of the following is *not* an element of the content analysis method employed by Demutrulias and Rosenthal?

    a. Intercoder reliability
    b. Instrument validation
    c. Sampling
    d. Focused interviews

3. Identify a strength of the content analysis method for assessing the existence of gender and racial stereotyping.

4. Identify a weakness of the content analysis method for assessing the existence of gender and racial stereotyping.

5. To what extent do you believe that the researchers' conclusions are supported by their data and the procedures which they employed in their research? Discuss.

6. To what extent does this study's content analysis design affect human subjects? Discuss.

Chapter 12

Tools and Data:
Using Historical Records to Expose the Myth of the Absent Family

Eugene D. Genovese (1986) utilized an historical research method to trace the development of black family forms over a period of time. This method usually involves an analysis of raw data from historical records. Typically, a researcher attempts to interpret the social life of a specific period by envisioning himself or herself in the circumstances of the people studied.

Genovese's interpretation of historical data on black family life during the period following the Civil War differed from that of many respected black and white historians and sociologists. He contended that too much emphasis had been placed on the historical continuity between families of slavery and those of twentieth-century black ghettos or inner cities. As a result, a myth evolved which held that both slaves and post-slavery blacks lacked a strong sense of family, as slavery had emasculated black men and led to the development of a matriarchal family structure.

Genovese also claimed that many researchers relied too much on slave laws as a source of data. Instead, he obtained data on the actual culture of the slave quarters from plantation records, diaries, and the correspondence of slaveholders. In addition, he drew upon the findings of other researchers based on evidence from the Civil War and Reconstruction eras, such as marriage certificates from the Union archives and slaveholders' wills.

Such data demonstrated to Genovese the need for a reassessment of slaves' family life which, he concluded, was more powerful than generally believed. He acknowledged the brutal pressures on blacks during slavery and the post-slavery period and suggested that his conclusions should be read within context—"as a record of the countervailing forces even within the slavocracy but especially within the slave community" (p. 30). He maintained that slaves created strong family norms which provided some semblance of a nuclear family structure, despite harsh conditions, and that they were able to sustain this remarkable stability within the post-war, white-dominated social system.

Genovese concluded that slaveholders were well aware of the importance of family life to their slaves. For example, plantation records revealed that one slaveholder considered the potential impact of selling a recalcitrant slave on the slave's family. To demonstrate the validity of this conclusion, Genovese drew from the actual quotes of plantation records, such as the following report made by slave overseer James W. Melvin to his employer Audley Clark Britton:*

> [Old Bill] breathed his last on Saturday the 31st, Jan., about 8-1/2 o'clock in the morning. He appeared prepared for Death and said he was going to heaven and wanted his wife to meet him there. When he took sick he told all it would be his last sickness—I was very sorry to lose him.

Besides reflecting on the closeness of spouses, the records describe many efforts by brothers and sisters and aunts and uncles to remain close to one another. Genovese tells of one brother who sneaked off to visit his sister on another plantation, despite the threat of whippings, of another brother who killed a slaveholder who murdered his sister, and of how widowed or abandoned slave women were looked after by siblings, nieces, nephews, and cousins.

According to Genovese, many slaveholders capitalized on the importance of family life to their slaves, as is evident in the writings of a Dutch slaveholder in Louisiana in the 1750s: "It is necessary that the Negroes have wives, and you ought to know that nothing attaches them so much to a plantation as children."

Some slaveholders took a somewhat paternalistic approach to dealing with their slaves, perhaps partly as a justification for owning other human beings. An example of this attitude may be found in the 1858 writings of William Massie of Virginia who, during a period of economic hardship, chose to sell his homestead rather than his slaves:

> To know that my little family, white and black, [is] to be fixed permanently together would be as near that thing happiness as I ever expect to get. . . . Elizabeth has raised and taught most of them and, having no children, like every other woman under like circumstances, has tender feelings toward them.

Other slave owners attempted to keep slave families together for economic reasons. Many slaves demanded this concession even while on the auction block,

---

*See Genovese's article, "The Myth of the Absent Family," in Robert Staples, (Ed.) 1986, *The Black Family: Essays and Studies,* Third Edition, Belmont, CA: Wadsworth Publishing Company, pp. 29-37, for citations of historical references, which are often scant and without dates.

at risk of severe punishment, which had a considerable effect on some masters. J. W. Metcalfe, for example, wrote to St. John R. Liddell that it was preferable to buy slaves in Virginia than in Louisiana, since it was easier to buy whole families who would work harder and be less troublesome if they were kept together.

Some slaveholders even took serious losses in order to buy an entire family. For example, John S. Wise described the case of a slave owner who was moved to buy an entire family rather than the husband and father alone by the pleading of Israel, a "crippled man of limited use," who would be separated from his wife and children if he were sold:

'Yes, sir, I kin do as much ez ennybody; and marsters, ef you'll only buy me and de chillum with Martha Ann, Gord knows I'll wuk myself to deth for you.' The poor little darkeys, Cephas and Melinda, sat there frightened and silent, their white eyes dancing like monkey-eyes, and gleaming in the shadows. As her husband's voice broke on her ear, Martha Ann, who had been looking sadly out of the window in a pose of quiet dignity, turned her face with an expression of exquisite love and gratitude towards Israel. She gazed for a moment at her husband and at her children, and then looked away once more, her eyes brimming with tears.

Of course, many less humane slaveholders asserted that slaves adjusted easily to separation from family members, despite their witnessing first-hand the terrible distress of family members who were forced apart. In the late period of slavery, several states attempted to forbid selling children separately from their mother, though only one state—Louisiana—did so.

Genovese concluded by asking, ". . . [C]ould any white Southerner pretend not to know from direct observation the meaning of Sojourner Truth's statement: 'I have borne thirteen chillun and seen 'em mos' all sold off into slavery, and when I cried out with a mother's grief, none but Jesus heard. . . .'"

ASSESSMENT QUESTIONS
for *Tools and Data,* Chapter 12

*Name*_____*Date*_____

Answer the following questions pertaining to the research on the development of black family forms by Eugene D. Genovese.

1. Which of the following research methods did Genovese use?

    a. survey research
    b. historical research
    c. content analysis
    d. evaluation

2. Which source of data was *not* used by Genovese?

    a. slave laws
    b. marriage certificates
    c. wills
    d. correspondence

3. Which quote does Genovese cite as evidence of slaveholders' desire to capitalize on their slaves' attachments to family members? Write out the quote and discuss how it demonstrates Genovese's point.

4. What type of historical record did Genovese use to determine that slaveholders knew that selling a recalcitrant slave had an impact on the slave's family?

   a. correspondence
   b. wills
   c. plantation records
   d. diaries

5. Genovese acknowledged that there was a range of motives among slaveholders for keeping the families of their slaves together. Comment on Genovese's interpretation of the remarks made by John S. Wise concerning Israel, a slave distressed at the prospect of being parted from his family. Do you agree with his view that the slaveholder in question bought the entire family for humane reasons? What other interpretation could be made?

6. Identify one way in which bias could be an important consideration in a researcher's examination of historical records, such as those discussed in this section.

Chapter 12

 Application:
Content Analysis Project

Name_____Date_____

Review a magazine with a focus on leisure pursuits, such as sports, travel, or hobbies. Analyze all the advertisements, illustrations, and photographs in which adults are portrayed to determine role expectations suggested in the print media. Include a variety of roles, such as working, playing, shopping, exercising, relaxing, and caring for children. Consider the following three variables in your analysis: sex, age group (late teens and 20's, 30's to 50's, 60's and over) and race/ethnicity (white, black, Asian, Hispanic, American Indian, and others).

Use the worksheets provided for your data analysis. Then report your findings by answering the following questions:

Name of Magazine_____

1. What is the size of the sample, i.e., the number of advertisements, pictures, and photographs portraying adults? (Refer to Worksheet #1.)

2. What is the percent distribution of your sample in terms of sex, age group, and race? (Refer to Worksheet #1.)

   Sex: Male_____ Female_____

   Age Group: Late teens and 20's_____ 30's to 50's_____ 60's and over_____

   Race: White_____ Black_____ Asian_____ Hispanic_____

   American Indian_____ Other_____

3. Identify five of the most common adult roles you found in your analysis. (Refer to Worksheet #2.)

_____

_____

_____

_____

_____

4. Indicate any of the role patterns that seem to vary by sex, age group or race/ethnicity. Explain. (Refer to Worksheet #2.)

Sex:

Age Group:

Race/Ethnicity:

5. State two latent (underlying) messages about adult roles that this magazine suggests.

   a.

   b.

6. Discuss your experience with the process of coding these data into sex, age group, and race/ethnicity variables. Indicate whether common sense or bias affected your coding decisions in any way.

Worksheet #1

Sample: Mark the *Frequency* column next to the appropriate category for each of the three variables, sex, age group, and race/ethnicity, as you see them in the magazine. Record the sum in the same column and the total frequency in the row labeled *Total*. Then calculate and record the percentages in the appropriate rows under the *Percent* column.

Variable	Frequency	Percent
Sex:		
Male	____	____
Female	____	____
Total	____	100%
Age Group:		
Late teens/20's	____	____
30's/50's	____	____
60's and over	____	____
Total	____	100%
Race/Ethicity:		
White	____	____
Black	____	____
Asian	____	____
Hispanic	____	____
American Indian	____	____
Other	____	____
Total	____	100%

Worksheet #2

Role Analysis: List the roles in the *Role* column. Mark the appropriate categories for sex, age group, and race/ethnicity for each role as you review the magazine. (Use the following key for the variable categories: Sex: M=Male, F=Female; Age Group: L=Late Teens/20's, M=30's/50's, H=60's and above; Race: W=White, B=Black, A=Asian, H=Hispanic American, Indian=AI, O=Other.)

Roles	Sex		Age Group			Race/Ethnicity					
	M	F	L	M	H	W	B	A	H	AI	O

Chapter 13

The Lab Work of the Social Researcher: Data Preparation

✔ *Research Brief:*

Coding Challenges of Unstructured Interviews

✔ *Tools and Data:*

'Dirty Data'

✔ *Application:*

Codebook Construction

Chapter 13

Research Brief:
Coding Challenges of Unstructured Interviews

As part of a qualitative study of sexual decisionmaking within the context of the AIDS epidemic, Karolynn Siegel and Beatrice J. Krauss (1991) conducted a study of 154 gay men—55 of whom were seropositive (HIV positive or in a pre-AIDS state of chronic illness), 41 who were seronegative, and 58 who were untested. The researchers used participant observation and self-administered questionnaires and conducted unstructured, individual interviews with a subsample of the 55 seropositive participants.

While the primary focus of the broader study was on sexual decisionmaking, the study involving the subsample of seropositive men dealt more with the problems they experienced in adapting to their HIV positive status. It became possible to discuss this unplanned topic during the interviews, because an open-ended questionnaire was used and the investigators did not specify a particular frame of reference. These two conditions are essential elements of the unstructructured interview, during which respondents are able to define the situation in their own terms and thus provide data that the researchers may not have anticipated.

The unstructured interview can be a more challenging technique to use than the structured interview. It requires greater skill on the part of the interviewer in order to ensure that sufficient data will be collected. Also, coding of the data may be more difficult due to a lack of standardization in question-and-answer formats.

Being aware of these concerns, Siegel and Krauss were especially careful in coding the interview material, so as to perform a secondary content analysis related to the respondents' problems in adapting to their HIV positive status. Each interview was audio-taped after the respondent viewed a discussion-stimulus video of five vignettes concerning gay men and their views on AIDS and safe sex. Transcripts were then prepared from the taped interviews. From these, in the researchers' own words,

. . . We developed a series of qualitative topic codes to facilitate content analysis of the data, beginning with an initial set of codes that reflected our provisional analysis of factors likely to be of theoretical importance in understanding the respondents' sexual adaptation to the threat of AIDS. This analysis was based primarily on the available literature, our own prior research, and our clinical experience with gay men at risk of HIV infection. As the data gathering proceeded, we refined and extended these codes to reflect and incorporate insights that emerged from the data.

The topic codes were inserted into the word processing file of each transcribed interview wherever textual material relevant to a factor appeared. Interrater agreement for assigning codes was assessed on a subsample of interviews and was found to be excellent for all but two of 22 topic codes. Disagreements on those codes were resolved by a third judge.

By using ZyIndex, a text-based software retrieval system, we could search the seropositve men's files for a topic code indicating comments relating to 'personal experience with HIV.' This material then was retrieved, stored in a separate file, and subjected to thematic analysis. . . . Two investigators derived eight themes independently from extracted material. Seven of these themes were identified by both individuals. An eighth theme was identified by one investigator and was corroborated by the other (pp. 20-21).

The researchers felt confident that the themes they had identified reflected the most relevant challenges facing their HIV-infected subjects, since they were brought out by the men themselves, either spontaneously and/or in response to general inquiries about their situations during unstructured interviews.

ASSESSMENT QUESTIONS
for *Research Brief,* Chapter 13

*Name*_____*Date*_____

Answer the following questions related to the study conducted by Siegel and Krauss.

1. Which form of interviewing is more conducive to ensuring a shared understanding of terms?

   a. structured
   b. unstructured

2. Which form of interviewing lends itself more readily to the coding of data?

   a. structured
   b. unstructured

3. The researchers used only those codes which they had developed prior to conduct- ing the interviews.

   a. True
   b. False

4. What was used in assessing interrater agreement for assigning codes?

   a. available literature
   b. a text-based software program
   c. a third rater
   d. a subsample of interviews

5. In addition to the interview material, what else did the researchers draw upon to develop their codes?

6. How did the researchers handle disagreements over the coding of the data?

7. Discuss how the consideration of ethics involved in working with human subjects could have been important in this study.

Chapter 13

Tools and Data:
'Dirty Data'

Name_____Date_____

This exercise applies to the stage in data preparation at which you have completed the coding and entered the data into the computer. After preliminary checks for data cleanliness, you have run the first statistical procedure on your computer analysis program and received a frequency distribution of the data. This initial statistical run is not performed for analysis, but as another step in error reduction. The output should be examined to insure that it is not "dirty data." Your common sense, as well as your sociological knowledge, is extremely important at this point.

Below is a portion of a questionnaire concerning youth activities and the frequency distribution output. Assume that this questionnaire was administered to a random sample of tenth-grade students in Beverly Hills, California, during the month of October, 1991.

Carefully examine the output for data which you suspect may be erroneous. (For example, a likely source for many such errors could be in the data entry itself.) Then enter your critique in the assessment area of the frequency distribution output. Identify the suspected error(s) for each variable listed and provide the reasons for your suspicion. For each variable which appears to have a believable frequency distribution, write "None" in the space provided for errors and enter your rationale in the space provided for reasons.

Youth Activities Questionnaire

V10
1. Male___(1)   Female___(2)

V11
2. Age____

V12
3. Race/Ethnicity
   White___(1)
   Black___(2)
   Hispanic___(3)
   Asian___(4)
   American Indian___(5)
   Other (Please specify.)_____(6)

V13
4. How would you best describe your family income?
   Below average___(1)
   Average___(2)
   Above average___(3)

5. What type of adult supervision is available in your home? (Check all that apply.)
   V14   Mother___
   V15   Father___
   V16   Other (Please specify.)_____

6. When during the week, if at all, do you usually spend time at home without any adults present?   (Check all that apply.)
   V17   Weekday afternoon___
   V18   Weekday evening___
   V19   Weekend morning___
   V20   Weekend afternoon___
   V21   Weekend evening___
   V22   Not at all, as there is always an adult present in my home___

V23
7. Do you currently have a job?
   Yes___(1) No___(2)

Frequency Distribution

V10	Sex:	(Valid Cases=100)

Value	Value Label	Valid Percent
1	Male	82%
2	Female	18%

Error(s):

Reason(s):

V11   Age (Expressed in years):   (Valid Cases=100)

Value   Valid Percent
10   10%
13   05%
15   60%
16   15%
17   05%
18   02%
19   02%
20   01%

Error(s):

Reason(s):

V12   Race/Ethnicity   (Valid Cases=90)

Value	Value Label	Valid Percent
1	White	25%
2	Black	50%
3	Hispanic	05%
4	Asian	05%
5	American Indian	10%
6	Other	05%

Error(s):

Reason(s):

V13   Family Income   (Valid Cases=80)

Value	Value Label	Valid Percent
1	Below Average	70%
2	Average	15%
3	Above Average	15%

Error(s):

Reason(s):

V14   Mother Available in Home (Valid Cases=100)

Value	Value Label	Valid Percent
1	Yes	25%
2	No	75%

Error(s):

Reason(s):

V15   Father Available in Home   (Valid Cases=100)

Value	Value Label	Valid Percent
1	Yes	85%
2	No	15%

Error(s):

Reason(s):

V16   Other Adult Available in Home   (Valid Cases=100)

Value	Value Label	Valid Percent
1	Yes	30%
2	No	60%

Error(s):

Reason(s):

V17   Home Without an Adult: Weekday Afternoon   (Valid Cases=100)

Value	Value Label	Valid Percent
1	Yes	70%
2	No	30%

Error(s):

Reason(s):

V18   Home Without an Adult: Weekday Evening (Valid Cases=100)

Value	Value Label	Valid Percent
1	Yes	50%
2	No	50%

Error(s):

Reason(s):

V19 Home Without an Adult: Weekend Morning (Valid Cases=100)

Value	Value Label	Valid Percent
1	Yes	70%
2	No	30%

Error(s):

Reason(s):

V20 Home Without an Adult: Weekend Afternoon (Valid Cases=100)

Value	Value Label	Valid Percent
1	Yes	50%
2	No	50%

Error(s):

Reason(s):

V21 Home Without an Adult: Weekend Evening (Valid Cases=100)

Value	Value Label	Valid Percent
1	Yes	70%
2	No	30%

Error(s):

Reason(s):

V22   Home Without an Adult: Not At All   (Valid Cases=100)

Value	Value Label	Valid Percent
1	Yes	100%
2	No	0%

Error(s):

Reason(s):

V23   Currently Have a Job   (Valid Cases=100)

Value	Value Label	Valid Percent
1	Yes	10%
2	No	90%

Error(s):

Reason(s):

Chapter 13

Application:
Codebook Construction

Name_____Date_____

A codebook serves as a directory for data. It provides detailed identifying information for labeling data, assigning codes, and designating locations for computer records. The content typically includes variable names, variable descriptions, response choices and their codes, and location.

Below is the structure of a sample codebook and an example using marital status. Instructions for completing this codebook are also provided. Review this information, then construct a codebook with the five variables provided.

CODEBOOK (*sample*)

Variable Name	*Variable and Values*	*Column(s)*
MAR	Marital Status	1
	(1) Married	
	(2) Single	
	(3) Divorced	
	(4) Widowed	
	(5) Separated	
	(9) Missing	

Variable Name: Select a short (less than 8 characters) name to identify the variable. This name can include letters and numbers but must begin with a letter. Some researchers use the prefix VAR and number their variables sequentially, i.e., VAR1, VAR2, VAR3. . . . Others use actual names, e.g., SEX, RACE, or abbreviations, e.g., MAR for marital status.

Variable: Describe the variable which appears on the questionnaire. For example, marital status, prestige ranking, employment status, and age (from date of birth). This description should be precise.

Value: The response choices and their codes should be listed here. For example, SEX could be listed as:

1	male
2	female
9	missing (if the respondent leaves the answer blank)

It is important to account for missing values. The number 9 is conventionally used to denote a missing value unless it stands for an actual code.

Column(s): This category indicates how much space to reserve in the computer, as well as the specific spaces to use: 1 to 9 response choices occupy a 1-digit space; 10 to 99 response choices occupy a 2-digit space; 100 to 999 response choices occupy a 3-digit space. For example, SEX is a one-digit code because there are two response choices—male or female. (Even if you allow for another category for missing data, in case the answer was left blank, the total number of categories will still be less than ten). If SEX is the first item in the codebook, it would occupy column 1. If the next variable is AGE, a 3-digit code would encompass all the possible responses (1 through 100+), so it would occupy columns 2 through 4.

Now construct a codebook in the space provided using the following five variables. Assign a variable name. Create response choices and codes, including a code for missing data. Determine the length of the variable and designate which columns it should occupy.

Employment Status—a variable which reflects whether the respondent is employed or not. If employed, the variable should be able to distinguish between part-time and full-time work.

Family Income—a variable that indicates an income range which best describes income earned by the family.

Religious Affiliation—a variable which provides response choices of major religious denominations as well as non-religious statuses, such as Atheist.

Frequency of Church Attendance—a variable which indicates how often the respondent attends church. A consistent time frame should be used, such as the number of times per month or times per year.

Political Affiliation—a variable which reflects the political party with which the respondent most closely identifies.

CODEBOOK

Variable Name   *Variable and Values*   *Column(s)*

Chapter 14

In Pursuit of Patterns: Data Analysis

✓ **Research Brief:**

Do 'Only Children' Have an Advantage?

✓ **Tools and Data:**

Stealing on the Job

✓ **Application:**

What Are the Trends?

Chapter 14

Research Brief:

Do 'Only Children' Have an Advantage?

Have those of you with siblings ever wondered how your life would have been different if you had been the "only child" in your family? Conversely, have any of you who are only children ever contemplated what might have been different if you had grown up with siblings?

Dudley Poston and Toni Falbo's (1990) research shed some light on this kind of speculation in their 1987 study of the only-child effect. Although most of the literature on only children is based on studies of Western children, Poston and Falbo's investigation used data collected from a sample of Chinese children. This approach helped to distinguish between universal tendencies and culturally-bound effects.

The sample consisted of 1,460 schoolchildren in the first and fifth grades in urban and rural areas of the Changchun metropolitan area. The researchers report that Changchun, a large industrial city located in the Jilin Province, is commonly viewed by the Chinese as a cross between Hollywood and Detroit because both movies and automobiles are produced there. The outlying areas of Changchun are mainly rural farmland.

Poston and Falbo selected two types of outcome variables for their research in order to determine whether only children ("onlies") differed significantly from children with siblings ("others") with respect to academic achievement and personality characteristics. Academic achievement included both math and verbal performance on examinations, as reported by teachers. Personality traits were identified as competence and virtue, as rated by parents (mostly mothers) and teachers. These personality characteristics were chosen as a result of their inclusion in earlier studies conducted in China, as well as the testing and advice of Chinese students pursuing graduate degrees at the University of Texas, Austin. Virtue and competence were measured as scales; virtue included such characteristics as gentleness, selflessness, modesty, and helpfulness, and competence included attributes such as confidence, competitiveness, leadership, and bravery.

Six independent variables were included as explanatory variables: (1) parental educational achievement, (2) only/other status, (3) gender, (4) parental help with homework, (5) parental expectations about the child's future, and (6) child-care arrangements prior to elementary school, i.e., nursery school or a relative's care. Subgroups of the data determined by grade level (1st or 5th grade) and residence (urban or rural) were created for some of the analysis, and interactions between only-child status and each of three variables (grade, gender, and residence) were also considered. (Interaction analysis permits researchers to combine variables, as in a male-only child or a female-only child.)

The researchers followed a two-step analysis plan. First, they looked at the effects of the only-child status (only versus other) on each of the six outcome variables: math achievement, verbal achievement, virtue by parental rating, virtue by teacher's rating, competence by parental rating, and competence by teacher's rating. This examination permitted them to determine the bivariate relationship between the only-child status and each of the outcome variables.

Bivariate analysis, which was the main strategy of previous studies of the only-child effect among Chinese children, may show a relationship between only-child status and variation in children's achievement and personality. Used alone, however, bivariate analysis can obscure the possible role of other variables, such as the educational level of the parents, in explaining the differences in achievement and personality. In addition, bivariate analysis alone is not always powerful enough to show significant results. In such a case, the interaction between two independent variables, such as only-child status and gender, can be useful. For example, male-only children might perform better on verbal achievement than others, while female-only children might perform similarly to others, or vice versa.

In view of the limitations of bivariate analysis, the researchers added a second step to their analysis plan—multivariate analysis. This procedure permits the consideration of the simultaneous contributions of additional independent variables. For this study, 48 multiple-regression equations were conducted to help determine the contributions and effects of the other independent variables.

The bivariate analysis revealed consistently significant differences between onlies and others with respect to achievement and some significant differences with respect to personality. These findings are summarized as follows:

- Onlies perform better than others on math achievement examinations.
- Onlies perform better than others on verbal achievement examinations.
- Teachers rate onlies as more virtuous than first-borns and second-borns from two-children households, and children third-born or higher from larger households.

The introduction of the other independent variables in the multivariate analysis step modified these initial findings. The math achievement advantage for the only-child held up for urban children, but not for rural ones. The verbal achievement advantage for onlies was even further restricted, pertaining solely to urban only-child first-graders, not to fifth-graders, nor to rural onlies from either grade. Furthermore, a direct comparison between onlies and first-borns revealed no significant differences in their achievement results.

The multivariate analysis also washed out the personality advantage detected in the simpler bivariate analysis. When additional independent variables were introduced as controls, the higher ratings of virtue bestowed by teachers on onlies diminished.

While this analysis reduced the advantage of only-child status, other variables consistently produced significant results in association with the outcome variables. The two most powerful explanatory variables were parental education and gender. Parental education significantly predicted academic achievement in 12 out of the 16 regression equations in which math or verbal achievement were analyzed. Similarly, gender significantly predicted virtue ratings in all 16 equations in which virtue was analyzed. (Girls were significantly more likely to be rated virtuous than were boys, regardless of grade level or urban/rural residence.)

Two additional variables worth noting in the multivariate analyses were early child-care status and parental expectations. Those children who had attended nursery school instead of being cared for by relatives were considered to be more virtuous in a number of equations, especially as rated by teachers. Nursery school participants were frequently viewed as more competent, as rated by teachers, as well. Variations in competency, as rated by parents, were significantly explained, in many cases, by parental expectations for their children's future.

Interestingly, there are more similarities than differences between the results of this research and the findings of studies conducted on Western samples. The most remarkable similarity is the advantage in academic achievement among only children noted in both the Chinese and Western samples. This advantage persisted, even when the effects of parental characteristics, gender, and nursery school attendance were taken into account. Another important similarity is the lack of personality differences between onlies and others, once additional control variables were introduced.

This study also noted an important distinction which had not been previously reported—the distinction between urban and rural only children.

The comparative survey methodology employed by Poston and Falbo was especially important to the contributions of research. First, its use of data from a non-Western nation such as China helped to place studies based primarily on Western nations into perspective. Second, its use of multivariate analysis improved on earlier research with Chinese samples. Finally, the comparative survey approach provided a systematic method for helping to distinguish between universal and culturally-specific tendencies regarding the only-child effect.

ASSESSMENT QUESTIONS
for *Research Brief,* Chapter 14

*Name*_____*Date*_____

Answer the following questions pertaining to the preceding research brief.

1. Which of the following variables is not an independent variable in Poston and Falbo's research?

   a. Gender
   b. Parental educational achievement
   c. Verbal achievement
   d. Parental help with homework

2. Which outcome variable was most consistently influenced by the effect of the only-child status?

   a. Virtue, as rated by the teacher
   b. Virtue, as rated by the parent
   c. Math achievement
   d. Competence, as rated by the parent
   e. All of the above

3. List two reasons why multivariate analysis provides more information than can be obtained from bivariate analysis alone.

   a.

   b.

4. State two modifications in the analysis which resulted from the introduction of the second step, multivariate analysis.

   a.

   b.

5. State two important contributions of Poston and Falbo's research.

   a.

   b.

6. Summarize Poston and Falbo's conclusions about the possible advantages of the only-child status.

7. Provide an interpretation of Poston and Falbo's finding that parental education had a more consistent bearing on achievement than did only-child status.

Chapter 14

Tools and Data:
Stealing on the Job

When a business executive takes a friend out to dinner and charges it to his or her business account, is that considered stealing? When an office worker takes home paper clips or memo pads and pens, is that worker stealing? What about the employee who makes personal long-distance phone calls on the company telephone—is he or she stealing? Is a factory worker stealing if he or she can produce 30 widgets per hour, but works at a slower pace to produce only 20? Finally, consider the taxi-cab driver who takes in $40 for a shift but reports only $25 to the boss—is there stealing going on here?

Research on workplaces has revealed that holding back on productivity, keeping part of the profit, taking supplies, and using employers' resources are commonplace across diverse occupations and settings (Coleman, 1989, Roethlisberger and Dickson, 1939, Roy, 1952, Vaz, 1984). Edmund W. Vaz's (1984) research on metropolitan taxi drivers in Montreal, Canada, provides an insightful example of this phenomenon.

Vaz's research was based on participant observational data collected over a four-year period, 1950-1955. During that period Vaz worked as a cab driver on various shifts for large and small employers. Thirty years later, during the early 1980s, informal conversations with cab drivers were held to confirm that the data still rang true.

Vaz gathered material from conversations with other drivers and employers. He estimated that his sample was between 95 and 100 drivers, in addition to several company executives, which he considered a "convenience sample" (non-probability sampling method). Verbatim conversations, as well as his personal impressions and observations, were recorded. In addition, 20 formal, two-hour interviews were conducted in Vaz's home or at the homes of the drivers.

Vaz concluded that stealing from employers is a well-established norm among cab drivers and, like other norms, expected behavior. Newcomers to the occupation are socialized into its practices. As a group, cab drivers apply sanctions on other employees to encourage compliance with the norm of stealing from their employers.

Below are some of the interview segments which Vaz cites as evidence of the stealing practices among the cab drivers he studied. Read the interviews and respond to the questions that follow. (Note that *Obs* stands for observer/interviewer in these segments.)

Segment A:

Obs: Why is a certain amount of stealing O.K.?

Boss: Why? Well, if they [drivers] take their lunch and cigarettes, it's O.K. You expect that. If they don't do it you know something is wrong. But don't take everything . . . .

Obs: Why do they steal in taxi work?

Boss: They are tempted too much. There is no control; they are tempted too much. But if you don't steal, the boss will still think that you steal. They figure that you steal off them. That's the business, that's the way they figure and they feel. You've got to do something.

Segment B:

Obs: Where did you first learn about stealing?

Driver: It depends how much the other guys made. If you make $30, you give him $18 or $20. I knew if I handed him too much, the other guys would gang up on me.

Obs: How?

Driver: Well, up there it's all one clique. They are working day in and day out. They more or less keep together. They did it to one guy. The guy was honest and he was handing in everything that he made. He used to have a car of his own. So they ganged up on him and they told him that he better stop handing in everything that he took in. "We'll fix you."

Segment C:

Obs: How do you know what to give him?

Driver: I ask the fellows. You hear the fellows talking in the garage and I give him the average . . . .

Obs: What did you do the first day that you drove?

Driver: I think the first couple of times I gave in all that I made. After three or four times, when I found out what the other guys were turning in, and that he wasn't checking the meter, I began doing the same thing.

Obs: When did you begin handing in less money than you actually took in?

Driver: About two months after I began working.

Obs: Why didn't you start the first day?

Driver: I didn't have enough experience and I didn't make good waybills. I was only making little waybills and the others were making $10 and more so I had to give him everything.

Obs: How did you come to learn about it?

Driver: We would talk on the stands and we would ask each other how much we had made. We would decide on the stands how much to hand in. It depended on what the speed was—$10, 12, 13.

Segment D:

Obs: How often do you steal?

Driver: Considering the cars I get and the reception I get with the waybill, I don't think I'm taking him for much. I'm giving him less than I actually earned.

Obs: Why?

Driver: I wouldn't make enough.

Obs: Do you think it is stealing?

Driver: It's never on my conscience. I've never taken 5 cents from somebody else. I earn that money when I'm out all night.

Obs: How much do you take?

Driver: I don't know because I don't keep track. I make about $28 and I give him $20-21. And I put gas in the car; I don't feel I'm gyping him. If anything goes wrong, I've got to pay. When the lights went out, I've got them fixed and I paid. If I left it up to the garage, he'd start yapping and raising hell. Instead of this, I take his money and pay anyhow.

Segment E:

Obs: What is your conception of a good taxi driver?

Driver: Somebody that stays on the job. That takes it easy on the car, doesn't drive too fast. If he breaks a spring, he will take it easy, doesn't goose her in first, and steals a little bit.

Obs: What do you mean "steals a little bit"?

Driver: Well, if he takes in $19, he cashes in $16, and if he takes in $24, he cashes in $20—steals with a heart."

ASSESSMENT QUESTIONS
for *Tools and Data,* Chapter 14

Name_____Date_____

Answer the following questions pertaining to the preceding research brief.

1. Consider the data from the first four interview segments (A, B, C, and D) and indicate which segment best matches each of the researcher's conclusions presented below.

   ____ The cab drivers regard their stealing with moral impunity.

   ____ New drivers become aware of the consequences of violating the norm and conform accordingly.

   ____ Socialization of new drivers into their work roles is gradual and often imperceptible.

   ____ Stealing is a normative part of the cab-driving occupation.

2. To what extent do you think that the data clearly support the interpretations stated in question #1?

   Explain.

3. Review segment D. Are the terms "stealing," used by the observer, and "take his money," used by the driver, significantly different?

   Explain.

4. Review segment E. State a plausible conclusion which could be reached from this interview segment.

5. To what population would you regard the findings of this research to be generalizable?

   Explain.

6. Describe a potential ethical problem posed by this study.

Chapter 14

Application:
What Are the Trends?

Name_____Date_____

Social researchers frequently analyze data that are obtained from federal agencies, such as the Bureau of the Census, the National Center for Health Statistics, and the Department of Health and Human Services. Two examples are presented below.

Example 1:

The National Center for Health Statistics provides data summaries on many topics, such as health, workforce participation, and family demographics, in its *Monthly Vital Statistics Report,* which is available free of charge. These summaries are frequently cited in textbooks in the social sciences, as well as used as supportive data in conducting research.

Below is a table adapted from the Annual Summary of *Births, Marriages, Divorces, and Deaths: United States, 1990* (National Center for Health Statistics, 1991). This table includes summary statistics of rates of birth, death, natural increase (the excess of births over deaths), marriage, divorce, and infant mortality for the years 1983-1990. Provisional rather than final rates are given for 1989 and 1990 as they had not yet been finalized. Note that the rates reflect the number per 1,000 people in the population, except for those pertaining to infant mortality which reflect the numbers of infant deaths per 1,000 live births.

Read over the table on the following page and answer the questions that follow.

Table A. Vital Statistics Rates: United States, 1983-90

[Infant mortality rates per 1,000 live births; all other rates per 1,000 population]

Rate[1]	1990 (prov)	1989 (prov)	1988 (fin)	1987 (fin)	1986 (fin)	1985 (fin)	1984 (fin)	1983 (fin)
Birth	16.7	16.2	15.9	15.7	15.6	15.8	15.5	15.5
Death	8.6	8.7	8.8	8.7	8.7	8.7	8.6	8.6
Natural Increase[2]	8.1	7.5	7.1	7.0	6.9	7.1	6.9	6.9
Marriage	9.8	9.7	9.7	9.9	10.0	10.1	10.5	10.5
Divorce	4.7	4.7	4.7	4.8	4.0	5.0	5.0	4.9
Infant Mortality	9.1	9.7	10.0	10.1	10.4	10.6	10.8	11.2

[1] Prov. refers to provisional; fin refers to final.
[2] The excess of births over deaths.

1. Between what two years did the birth rate increase the most?

   a. 1989 and 1990
   b. 1984 and 1985
   c. 1957 and 1958
   d. 1988 and 1989

2. Which rate showed a slight increase in 1990, following a steady decline?

   a. divorce
   b. marriage
   c. infant mortality
   d. death

3. Which rate has been the most stable, i.e., has shown the least fluctuation, between 1983 and 1990?

   a. divorce
   b. marriage
   c. infant mortality
   d. death

4. Which rate has been the least stable, i.e., has shown the most fluctuation, between 1983 and 1990?

    a. divorce
    b. marriage
    c. infant mortality
    d. death

5. Indicate one possible reason for the large gain in the natural increase rate between 1989 and 1990.

6. Which rate do you find surprising in terms of either its fluctuation or general stability over the eight years? Discuss.

Example 2:

The U.S. Department of Health and Human Services publishes pamphlets and reports on a multitude of topics. One such report is *Aging America: Trends and Projections—1987-88 Edition*, which was was prepared by the U.S. Senate Special Committee on Aging in conjunction with the American Association of Retired Persons, the Federal Council on the Aging, and the U.S. Administration on Aging.

The table presented on the following page shows the rates of poverty among elderly and non-elderly adults for the years 1959-1986. The rates reflect the percentage among the specific population.

Read over the table and answer the questions that follow.

Table B. Poverty Rates for Elderly and Non-Elderly Adults: 1959 to 1986

	Poverty Rate	
Year	18 to 64	65 plus
1959	17.4	35.2
1966	10.6	28.5
1967	10.2	29.5
1968	9.1	25.0
1969	8.8	25.3
1970	9.2	24.5
1971	9.4	21.6
1972	9.0	18.6
1973	8.5	16.3
1974	8.5	14.6
1975	9.4	15.3
1976	9.2	15.0
1977	9.0	14.1
1978	8.9	14.0
1979	9.1	15.2
1980	10.3	15.7
1981	11.3	15.3
1982	12.3	14.6
1983	12.1	14.1
1984	11.7	12.4
1985	12.1	14.1
1986	11.7	12.4

Source: Congressional Research Service with 1985
and 1986 data supplied by U.S. Bureau of the Census.

1. Which year showed the greatest difference in the poverty rate between elderly and non-elderly adults?

   a. 1959
   b. 1967
   c. 1973
   d. 1986

2. Which year showed the least difference in the poverty rate between elderly and non-elderly adults?

a. 1975
b. 1978
c. 1984
d. 1986

3. Which year began to show a reversal of a trend in the poverty rates of non-elderly adults?

   a. 1972
   b. 1978
   c. 1983
   d. 1985

4. Which group—elderly or non-elderly—showed a greater decrease in the poverty rate between 1959 and 1986?

   a. elderly
   b. non-elderly

5. Looking over this table, what trends in poverty rates for both the elderly and non-elderly would you predict in the years following 1986? Indicate the reasons for your predictions.

   Elderly:

   Non-elderly:

6. Indicate one possible reason for the large decline in the poverty rate among the elderly from 1959 through 1986.

Chapter 15

'As I Was Saying. . .': Communication of Findings

✓ *Research Brief:*

Contrasting Two Approaches

✓ *Tools and Data:*

'We Do Not, At This Time, Offer Any Solutions. . .'

✓ *Application:*

Scholarly Journals Versus Magazines

Chapter 15

Research Brief:
Contrasting Two Approaches

In a 1987 article in the journal *Educational Evaluation and Policy Analysis,* Patricia Haensly, Ann Lupkowski, and James McNamara address the importance of effectively communicating research findings to practitioners and policymakers. Even the best research, they contend, will not have the impact it should, unless its implications are clearly understood by those concerned. The writers suggest that the best way to reach both scientists and non-scientists is to present two different research reports: a traditional, methods-oriented report that follows the conventions dictated by science and an application-oriented report that emphasizes specific findings rather than general methodology and hypothese

To illustrate the basic elements of both types of research reports, Haensly and her colleagues contrast a "chart essay" (a report form under development at Texas A&M University by McNamara and the EPSY Survey Research Group [1983], among others) with a methods-oriented report from a survey on the extracurricular activities of 515 Texas high school seniors (McNamara, Haensly, Lupkowski, and Edline, 1985).

Designed to accompany oral briefings to policymakers and/or practitioners, the chart essay displays a sequential development of the study through a series of charts. Table 1 below shows the relationship between the basic elements of the two types of research reports.

Table 1

Contrast of Methods-Oriented versus Policy-Oriented Reports

Method-Oriented Report	Chart Essay
Problem statement	Design of the inquiry
Theoretical framework	
Review of the literature	Prior research
Hypotheses	Personal beliefs

Method-Oriented Report	Chart Essay
Methods	
Subjects	Sampling design
Measures	Questionnaire design
Results	Findings on specific research questions
Discussion	
Policy recommendations	Implications for practice
Research recommendations	Future research

Typically, the charts address the eight concerns found in the right column of Table 2 below.

Table 2

Elements of a Chart Essay and Corresponding Questions

Chart Essay	General Research Question
Problem statement	What was the general research question that guided this study?
Theoretical framework	
Prior research	Why was this study conducted?
Hypotheses	What did we expect to find in this study?
Methods	
Sampling design	Who were the subjects in this study?
Questionnaire design	How was the impact of extracurricular activities on learning measured?
Results	What were the findings of this study?
Discussion	
Policy implications	What are the implications of this study for policymakers and practitioners?
Future research	As a result of this study, what directions can be advanced for future research?

An example of a chart essay corresponding to one of the eight concerns is found in Figure 1 on the following page.

Figure 1

Chart 1 of the TAMU Chart Essay on the Role of Extracurricular Activities

Design of the Inquiry

The major purpose of this inquiry was to examine the impact of high school extracurricular activities on learning.

The three specific tasks for this inquiry were:

- To determine if more involvement in extracurricular activities is linked with academic achievement.
- To describe the extracurricular participation and academic achievement of award-winning students and student leaders.
- To provide descriptive data pertaining to students' beliefs regarding the benefits of extracurricular participation.

*   *   *

This investigation was designed to provide answers for the following 15 research questions:

Research Question 1: In what extracurricular activities are high school students most likely to participate?

Research Question 2: How actively involved are high school students in the extracurricular activities they select?

Research Question 3: Does participation in athletics contribute significantly to academic success in high school?

Research Question 4: Does participation in career clubs contribute significantly to academic success in high school?

Research Question 5: Does participation in communications contribute significantly to academic success in high school?

Research Question 6: Does participation in career clubs contribute significantly to academic success in high school?

Research Question 7: Does participation in the honor society contribute significantly to academic success in high school?

Research Question 8: Does outside work in out of school youth organizations contribute significantly to academic success in high school?

Research Question 9:   Does participation in outside work contribute significantly to academic success in high school?

Research Question 10: Does participation in service organizations contribute significantly to academic success in high school?

Research Question 11: Does participation in student government contribute significantly to academic success in high school?

Research Question 12: Does participation in all extracurricular activities contribute significantly to academic success in high school?

Research Question 13: Are the number of awards won and the number of leadership roles held a determinant of academic success in high school?

Research Question 14: In what extracurricular activities are student leaders and award-winning students most likely to participate?

Research Question 15: What are the benefits of participation in extracurricular activities as perceived by the students?

ASSESSMENT QUESTIONS
for *Research Brief,* Chapter 15

Name_____Date_____

Answer the following questions pertaining to methods-oriented and policy-oriented research reports as described in the preceding research brief.

Match the items listed below with the type of report in which they appear by marking either *a* for a methods-oriented report or *b* for a chart essay report in the spaces provided.

1. _____ theoretical framework

2. _____ hypotheses

3. _____ implications for practice

4. _____ problem statement

5. _____ measures

6. _____ personal beliefs

7. _____ in-person presentation

8. _____ written journal article

9. _____ subjects

10. _____ prior research

11. For what type of audience is the chart essay research report designed?

    a. basic researchers
    b. policymakers and practitioners
    c. scientific journal readers
    d. all of the above

12. What is one major advantage of the chart essay research report over the traditional methods-oriented report?

Discuss.

Chapter 15

Tools and Data:
'We Do Not, At This Time, Offer Any Solutions. . .'

A research report issued in June of 1991 by The State of Washington's Children sparked controversy among child advocates regarding both the data and the manner in which they were presented (*Seattle Post-Intelligencer,* June 14, 1991 and June 18, 1991). The report was prepared by The Washington Child Health Research and Policy Group, a group of academicians, public officials, health care professionals and child welfare advocates who collected data over a two-year period on 25 indicators affecting the lives of the state's children, including family composition, poverty, youth suicide, teen motherhood, infant mortality, and substance abuse. In addition, experts were surveyed using a "Delphi Technique" that "distills expert judgment on a particular topic" (Washington Child Health Research and Policy Group, 1991, p. 3). The stated intent of the study was to compare children in Washington state with those in the rest of the nation in order to obtain information on problems and promising trends that could assist policymakers, community leaders, and others in making informed decisions.

The report was widely criticized. Critics complained that it tended to mask the real decline in child welfare in the state and nation and failed to provide concrete suggestions for improvement. They suggested that the report offered more congratulations than concern over continuing and worsening problems. The Delphi Technique was also criticized.

Much of this criticism was based on the contents of a "summary report" issued to provide a concise overview of the findings detailed in the actual report. It was this report that most people, including the media, received and which elicited the most adverse response. What was in the summary report that provoked such a negative reaction?

The report contained the following sections:

- Who are our children?
- What are the issues?
- How are we doing?
- What is being done?
- What can be done?

The space allotted for each section is significant. The longest section (3 pages) was on the topic "How are we doing?" and includes the following points:

- The good news is that Washington's children appear to be better off than children in the rest of the nation.
- More good news is that some indicators reflecting the health of these children are improving.
- The bad news is that conditions in Washington state have grown worse, compared to a generation ago.
- In regard to some of the problems measured, Washington's children do worse than the rest of the nation.
- In virtually all areas, there is a persistent disparity between rich and poor, white and non-white.

The "What is being done?" section (2-1/2 pages) listed 15 programs administered or supported by the state and/or federal government. However, the "What can be done?" section (1/3 of a page) contained only three short paragraphs:

These programs are important steps in the right direction. But, by most accounts, much more needs to be done.

This first report only begins to document the state of our children. We have compiled much [sic] data, but much more is not yet available, and that leaves some gaps in our knowledge. Also, while we hope the information in this report adds to an understanding of the challenges and problems faced by children—and thus leads to better decisions on their behalf—*we do not, at this time, offer any solutions* (italics added).

Public and private decisionmakers must continue to focus efforts and resources on the long-term needs of Washington's children—healthy and stable families, vibrant and economically viable communities, affordable housing, quality schools and accessible health and social services—while still improving their ability to overcome the here-and-now challenges of domestic violence, drugs, hunger, injuries and social dysfunction. Everybody has a stake in the success of these efforts.

While critics charged that the summary report contained nothing new and even served to support the argument that improvements are unnecessary (Charles Langdon, former Director of the Children's Home Society, as quoted in the *Seattle Post-Intelligencer,*

June 14, 1991), those involved in the research had a different view. For example, Dr. Maxine Hayes, Assistant Secretary of the Parent-Child Health Services for the state's Department of Health, argued that the group did not want their findings to generate despair rather than action. She said, "We didn't want to come in with gloom and doom. . . . It's really not as bad here as it is in other places. . . . We can take control of the problems now that are manageable" (Seattle Post-Intelligencer, June 14, 1991). Another research group member, Dorothy Mann, Regional Administrator for the federal Public Health Services, suggested that the report should be used as a "catalyst for others to take action" (*Seattle Post-Intelligencer,* June 14, 1991).

Regardless of whether or not criticisms of the summary report's content were justified, it is unfortunate that the manner in which it communicated the study's findings appeared to attract as much, if not more, attention than the findings themselves.

ASSESSMENT QUESTIONS
for *Tools and Data*, Chapter 15

Name_____Date_____

Answer the following questions pertaining to the June, 1991, State of Washington's Children Summary Report.

1. What type of data collection method was used in the study?

   a. survey
   b. participant-observation
   c. content analysis
   d. experiment

2. Which section of the Summary Report did critics believe should have received more attention?

   a. Who are our children?
   b. What are the issues?
   c. How are we doing?
   d. What is being done?
   e. What can be done?

3. What was the critics' main complaint about the summary report?

4. What was the main defense offered by the research group?

5. What is one thing the research group could have done differently in presenting its findings?

Chapter 15

Application:
Scholarly Journals versus Magazines

Name_____Date_____

In this exercise you will contrast two different types of research reports: 1) a scientific presentation of research found in an academic journal that is geared toward the scholar; and 2) a "pop sociology" type of article from a popular magazine that is geared toward the lay reader.

Procedure:

1. Visit your college library and select two articles to compare: one from a scholarly journal in sociology, e.g., *American Sociological Review, American Journal of Sociology, Sociology of Education,* or other social science, e.g., *Sex Roles, The Gerontologist, Journal of Applied Behavioral Science, American Psychologist*; the second from a popular magazine containing articles on social research, *e.g., Psychology Today, Ms. Magazine, Atlantic Monthly, The New York Times Magazine, The New Yorker, National Geographic.* The articles selected should pertain to studies of sociological interest, using sociological research methods.

2. List the journal and magazine and the titles of the articles you selected.

    Scholarly Journal: Popular Magazine:

3. After reading the articles, list the major headings and subheadings of each.

Scholarly Journal   Popular Magazine

Major Headings: Major Headings:

Subheadings: Subheadings:

4. Record the following information for each article:
What percentage of the article space is devoted to research design and methods? (Specify whether space is measured in terms of paragraphs or pages.)

Scholarly Journal _____   Popular Magazine _____

5. What percentage of the article space is devoted to results/findings? (Specify whether space is measured in terms of paragraphs or pages.)

Scholarly Journal _____   Popular Magazine _____

6. Are specifics of the sample selection detailed? (Yes or No)

Scholarly Journal _____   Popular Magazine _____

7. Is a survey of the literature included? (Yes or No)

Scholarly Journal _____   Popular Magazine _____

8. Are recommendations for future research included? (Yes or No)

   Scholarly Journal _____   Popular Magazine _____

Analysis:

9. What are two main differences in the articles?

   a.

   b.

10. Which article is easier to understand? Why?

11. Which article is more believable? Why?

 Chapter **16**

Spotlight on Social Researchers

Peter Rossi, Stuart A. Rice Professor of Sociology
  University of Massachusetts, Amherst

Howard S. Becker, Professor of Sociology
  University of Washington

Maxine Baca Zinn, Professor of Sociology
  Michigan State University

James Davis, Professor of Sociology, *Harvard University*
  Research Associate, *National Opinion Research Center*

Morris Rosenberg (deceased), formerly Professor of Sociology
  University of Maryland

Pauline Bart, Professor of Sociology, Department of Psychiatry,
  University of Illinois, Chicago

Oswald Hall, Professor Emeritus, Department of Sociology
  University of Toronto

James Coleman, Professor of Sociology and Education
  University of Chicago

Chapter 16

Spotlight on Social Researchers

This chapter takes you behind the scenes of social research to acquire an inside view of the human experiences of researchers. During 1990-91, we conducted telephone interviews with several prominent social researchers*, asking them to reflect on their roles as researchers and answer such questions as "What initially excited you about social research? How do you go about choosing your research topics?" and "What has been your greatest research challenge and how did you deal with it?"

Their responses to the interview questions demonstrated a wide range of motivations, interests, and experiences. Some are highly mathematical in their work, while others analyze observational and interview material. One researcher started out to be a journalist, another began as a social worker, another was seeking answers to a personal family matter, and yet another wanted to increase our knowledge about families of various races and ethnicities. One researcher found his research topics virtually by accident, ranging from medical students to the sociology of art. Others chose their topics based on long-standing interests, such as self-esteem and marginalized people.

Despite their differences, all our subjects expressed great enthusiasm about their work as a social researcher. Before reading the following interviews, you should be aware that their enthusiasm can be contagious. If so, remember that invitation you received from Results, Inc. They are waiting for your reply.

---

*Conscientious, deliberate efforts were made in our selection of social researchers based on gender, age, and race/ethnicity. While not totally successful in our efforts, the ones included do reflect some level of diversity. Where we were more successful was in achieving a balance between qualitative- and quantitative- as well as basic- and applied-oriented approaches.

PETER ROSSI, Stuart A. Rice Professor of Sociology,
University of Massachusetts, Amherst

". . . it took me about four or five years to convince President Kennedy's Commission on Crime to support a pilot study which would illustrate the extent to which victimization surveys would be useful in the study of the incidence of crime."

Interviewer: What initially excited you about social research?

Rossi: The initial excitement was that there was something that could be technically extremely challenging and at the same time productive of results which might be beneficial to society. So it is a combination of both.

Initially, I was oriented toward social work as an undergraduate and very much interested in contributing to the solution of social problems. Then I took a research methods course as an undergraduate. I began to see there was another way I could make a contribution and that would be to provide basic knowledge that would be useful in the devising of beneficial social policy. So, in other words, I'm a busy body.

Interviewer: How have you typically gone about picking your research topics?

Rossi: There are two versions to that. Version number one is influenced a great deal by the availability of funds to support research. Version number two says that the important thing to do is to go out and make the opportunities. So it is a combination of both.

That is to say, with respect, for example, to the work which I did on the development of victimization surveys. It took me about four or five years before I was able to convince President Kennedy's Commission on Crime to support a pilot study which would illustrate the extent to which victimization surveys would be useful in the study of the incidence of crime. So it is a combination of opportunities plus making the opportunities or fashioning the availability of funds to pursue research topics of my interest.

Interviewer: How did you finally convince them?

Rossi: I started out trying to convince private foundations and one of them was interested, as well as the National Science Foundation and The National Institute of Health. One of things, if you want to pursue a strategy of this sort, is that you can never be daunted by people saying no to you. I guess go back and steel yourself for getting turned down repeatedly.

Interviewer: Have you had an intriguing research challenge that you had to find a clever way to solve?

Rossi: Counting the homeless. That is difficult because the conventional ways of undertaking sample surveys, or censuses for that matter, is to make the assumption that everybody in the United States, if you are doing a survey in the United States, has an address. By definition, that is not true for the homeless, so I had to devise what turned out to be the photographic negative of the conventional method in which we sampled not addresses, but nonaddresses.

The sample survey which I did in Chicago involved taking a sample of blocks in the Chicago area and searching those blocks in the middle of the night. Anyone we found who was outside a conventional [dorming] unit, we questioned them as to whether or not they had a conventional [dorming] unit to go to. This method provides an unbiased estimate of people who are out in the middle of the night and who have no addresses to go to. When you add that to another sample of people in the emergency shelters, you get a relatively good sample capable of being the basis for an estimate of the homeless by combining the two samples with proper weight and so on.

Interviewer: As you have done a lot of evaluation research, overall, what has been your approach to communicating findings?

Rossi: That has been my most serious failure. I am really more interested in doing the research than in communicating findings. The major piece of evaluation research I did, which was randomized experiments with released prisoners, resulted in a monograph describing the experiment and its findings. But there was no attempt on my part to put this into operation as a standing procedure.

It seems to me that skills that are involved in communicating research findings to a wide audience, either of a popular variety or of the Congress, which would be relevant to the case of the research I did, are really different skills. And I don't have the patience for spending a lot of time in meetings. If you have the patience for it, then you may not have the time to do the research. I prefer the research. I hope it has some impact.

HOWARD S. BECKER, Professor of Sociology, University of Washington

"Doing research is a little bit like Sherlock Holmes. The only difference is that you get to make up the puzzles."

Interviewer: First, what initially excited you about social research?

Becker: When I just finished my undergraduate work, I read a book called *Black Metropolis* by Horace Cayton with St. Clair Drake. It was a big anthropological study of the south side of Chicago. I thought that was just terrific—the urban anthropologist at work. I thought that was really great, in the sense that Sociology had all the components of Anthropology. Then I went to graduate school. And in graduate school, those naive ambitions and impulses get trained and socialized into something professional. So you learn to do it the way the rest of them do it.

Interviewer: What has kept you involved in it?

Becker: Doing research, how should I describe it, is a little bit like Sherlock Holmes. The only difference is that you get to make up the puzzles. You don't always know what the question is, and somehow, you have to go about working it out.

A bunch of years ago, I did a study with some colleagues on medical students. Actually, when we started, we really did not have a problem, you know, hypothesis testing. We said to ourselves, "Students come in [to medical school] on one end without knowledge and training, and they were expected to know quite a lot about medicine by the time they reach the other end. Something must happen along the way. What?

What we began to see—the interesting problem for us was not what they learned but how they resisted learning. This problem brought us eventually to the idea of students working together to define learning. The students had an anatomy book that was three inches thick and they were expected to know everything in it. Well, they quickly learned that the most important thing was to pass the test. This will not be unfamiliar to you. Therefore, they had to figure out what was going to be on the test. This became their way, not of evading learning, but of focusing what they had to do.

Interviewer: How do you go about choosing your research topics?

Becker: By accident. I did not choose to work with medical students. Rather, I was looking for work and a colleague of mine had received a grant to look at medical students. Part of becoming a professional is that you learn to get interested in problems even if you are not interested in them for their own sake. After we had done this research on medical students, we then had a connection at the University of Kansas and in the Sociology of Education which led to other projects.

In 1970, I just got tired of studying education. I knew the education officer in Rio de Janeiro, and he called me up and said, "There is someone down here who knows your work. Why don't you come down here and teach."

I wish I could say that I've picked all these topics and opportunities for good, rational reasons, but I didn't. In fact, I don't wish I could say that.

Now, I have become interested in the Sociology of Art because I have a lot of friends in the art community.

Interviewer: Have you had any ethical dilemmas that you have had to overcome?

Becker: In the work that I do, the way that question comes up is never with the people I am studying, but with the people who preside over them. In one case, we had this argument with the Dean of the Medical School. For instance, with the *Boys in White* research, we reported that "many" of the medical students did the work of externs. An extern is like a junior intern. An extern, unlike an intern, is not licensed to practice under hospital staff and does not have responsibility to make medical decisions. Well, the Dean did not like this term, and therefore, didn't like the suggestion that "many" of their students had done this work. So we changed the word from "many" to "some." Many includes some, and we did not know for sure because we didn't ask this question of all students. We didn't ask every tenth student, for instance, "Are you working as an extern?" It was a minor issue, and when the student mentioned it, we recorded it. Of course, this finding got at what we found out about the way medical students were treated. The implication of the title *Boys in White*, which was imbedded in the analysis, is that they are being treated as children.

MAXINE BACA ZINN, Professor of Sociology, Michigan State University

"The problem I am talking about and I will put it bluntly, is 'Was I biased? Was I biased about the way I wanted the data to come out and be presented?'"

Interviewer: What initially excited you about social research?

Baca Zinn: The most immediate answer to that has to do with my own racial/ethnic identity and the way that I was learning Sociology as an undergraduate student and the real fascination I had with the "big picture." Seeing the big picture, I was taught that I could understand myself, and my life, and the world around me. That explanation and that approach didn't apply to racial/ethnic people, and it didn't apply to racial/ethnic families. And yet I saw people all around me producing knowledge really, and producing ideas, and finding out things about the world in which they lived and they weren't finding out what I considered to be the right answers about, in my case, Mexican-American people, and other people of color. So I was struck by this real disjuncture between the standard sociological approach, looking at things in terms of the big picture, and then the approach used to study racial/ethnic people which was an approach that hinged on culture. So this disjuncture excited me. I thought, I guess, I was naive enough or brave enough to think that I could do research that would set the record straight as far as people of color were concerned.

Interviewer: Do you find that the topics you study, especially ethnicity, gender, and family have an effect on the type of research strategies you use?

Baca Zinn: I do indeed. I started out with an alternative conceptual approach. I thought that in addition to looking at racial/ethnic families, and I will talk specifically about Latino families because most of my research focused on Latino families, I thought that not only did we need an alternative conceptual approach and different questions that outsiders hadn't been asking, but it needed to be posed by insiders like me who saw this gap between our lives and what sociologists were saying about us. I thought that we needed a different methodological approach.

So I chose field methods in my earliest research on Chicano families because I thought it would enable me to tap backstage behaviors, to pose questions, and to get at areas of the family that remained obscure to outsiders, to Anglo scholars, and to those who were using more detached methods. Given the private nature of family life in this society, I thought I had to find a way to get inside of family life. So my methodological strategy was to use interviews combined with participant observation.

Interviewer: What ethical dilemmas in social research have you had to overcome?

Baca Zinn: I was especially concerned with the idea of minority research as exploitation. There has been so much concern in minority communities that outsiders—researchers, Anglos—come in and study their communities and leave without giving anything in return, and furthermore, putting the knowledge that they take from their communities to dubious use, i.e., more and further descriptions that are pejorative in describing their place and their location in the social world. I was really concerned as a minority researcher that not take place.

I think it was hard to do that given what I wanted to do. It was hard to establish complete reciprocity because, after all, I was the researcher—in some ways the outsider—although I became an insider who came in, and wanted information, and controlled the interaction, and posed the questions and ultimately had the power in this relationship. I think that I didn't change the power dimension, but I did everything I could do to ensure reciprocity.

I went into the field wanting a more correct presentation of Latino family life. In some ways I was partial to a more accurate presentation of Latino families, and, for me, in some ways it was an overarching problem. The problem I am talking about, and I will put it bluntly, is "Was I biased?" Was I biased about the way in which I wanted the data to come out and to be presented. I really struggled with that problem, and now it has a name. The name I found for this concept years and years later is "conscious partiality." It is a term for a researcher in my situation, that is a researcher who is not a completely detached observer. I was partial to a more balanced portrayal of Chicano families.

Interviewer: Do you see critical changes between now and then [the seventies] in the sense of a student coming into the field now?

Baca Zinn: Yes. I think, if anything, especially for minorities and women that are coming into the field and have some fundamental questions about the presentation and explanations about their people. I think we are far more sophisticated. I think we ask far better questions. I think that our methodological sophistication has advanced far beyond what it was at the time that I began [the seventies] so I think times are far better. I think there has never been a better time to be a sociologist and to ask questions about social location and marginalized people.

JAMES DAVIS, Professor of Sociology, Harvard University, and Research Associate, National Opinion Research Center (NORC)

"I work on national surveys, and I am always just very eager to see what's happening, what's going on, what differences there are, what trends there are."

Interviewer: What initially excited you about social research?

Davis: I came at it from journalism. As an undergraduate I studied journalism and was very active in newspapers and student magazines. I got involved in some survey that was done by a student magazine, and I got interested in research because it seemed to me social research was intrinsically more interesting than journalism. It went beyond the day-to-day superficialities, and you could look at more general sorts of issues and findings. I had worked on a newspaper and found it kind of fun, but every day was a new day and there never seemed to be any patterns. But in social research you could look for patterns, perhaps something more ambitious than a news report on a particular event.

Interviewer: What has kept you involved in the field?

Davis: I do it, in part, for the money because I get a little extra money for my research and, in part, just plain curiosity. I work on national surveys, and I am always just very eager to see what's happening, what's going on, what differences there are, what trends there are. Also, after you have been at it a while you have sort of a reputation you want to defend or show off so you publish your results to show people you are alive.

Interviewer: What has been the greatest challenge for you in conducting surveys?

Davis: Getting the money. My main research is a project at the National Opinion Research Center [NORC] of the University of Chicago. It has been going on for 20 years. It is a fairly large scale continuing project which is quite different from firing off a proposal to do this and do that. It has been funded by the National Science Foundation, and they have been very generous over a couple of decades. But, our project takes up a large proportion of the sociology budget of the National Science Foundation and there is always a question whether they should support a unique project like this or individual studies. We argue that since our project makes data available to the whole profession, it is beneficial to everybody.

Interviewer: What type of surveys does NORC do?

Davis: It is a general sort of department store of social research. It does anything for anybody. Its specialty is very, very large scale, very detailed surveys particularly in the evaluation of government programs—health care and educational programs and the like.

The aim of my project, the GSS [General Social Survey], is to make data widely available, and in terms of our success in making the data available to other researchers, I think we have been extremely successful. We have a bibliography of over 2000 citations of people who have done research using data from the program. It has evolved into an international program, and there are now something like 15 nations that have similar studies.

Interviewer: Has there been one project that you have found to be especially enjoyable?

Davis: The most generally rewarding experience has been this general social survey project that has gone on a long time and had a certain amount of impact. The most fun probably was the very first study I did at NORC which was an evaluation of the Great Books Program. The Great Books Program is an adult education program in which people meet weekly and read Plato and Aristotle and stuff like that and develop a liberal arts education. NORC was hired to do an evaluation of the program, and I just happened to be the person assigned to the project. I had a lot of fun. I got a free trip to Aspen, Colorado to watch the Great Books in action. I wrote what I thought was a wonderful book called *Great Books in Small Groups* about how small group processes affect adult education. It was not a great success, but I felt happy about it.

Interviewer: What ethical dilemmas in social research have you had to overcome?

Davis: Oddly enough, I can't recall myself being caught in an ethical dilemma involving my research. In the sort of research we do there are very definite ethical standards, and well thought out issues, for instance, confidentiality. One problem that is fairly common is when an interviewer stumbles upon a very serious family problem. She discovers that the husband is beating the wife, which might come out in an interview. But what are her ethical obligations—should she inform somebody? On the other hand, that information is confidential.

So that sort of problem does turn up in survey research in general. I myself have never encountered any. I don't want to sound morally obtuse, but these issues have been pretty well thought out by the profession, and if one follows the professional guidelines, you are very seldom caught in ethical dilemmas.

MORRIS ROSENBERG, Professor of Sociology, University of Maryland

"I just don't believe what people say. Given my awareness of how their biases are going to govern their judgements and so on, I simply have to have evidence."

Interviewer: What initially excited you about social research?

Rosenberg: When I came into sociology as a graduate student, I was not oriented toward research. I was oriented toward theory. Frankly, my feeling about methodology was something that I had to get through, but it wasn't really a primary interest of mine.

In the course of my training, I became exposed to research, and I guess my interest was mostly aroused by my professor, Paul Lazarsfeld, who was the most brilliant researcher I think that has ever come out of sociology. In time, I became his assistant. But in the process, I could see the excitement involved in solving methodological problems and thinking causally about the relationships among variables and so on. It became inherently fascinating. I found it something new, something unexpected. It had a fairly tight logic which appealed to me.

Interviewer: What has kept you involved in the field?

Rosenberg: What kept me in it—many factors are obviously involved. Basically it becomes circular. You get into research, you do research, you get funded to do more research, and you continue on. I have always done research to solve problems and ask questions to learn more about things.

Also, the longer I spent in sociology, the more jaundiced I became about the bias of my colleagues—their reluctance to let facts stand in the way of their conclusions, their willingness to generalize on the basis of individual cases, and so on. Frankly, I found that irritating; I found it annoying; and I found their indifference to facts to be disturbing. I just don't believe what people say. Given my awareness of how their biases are going to govern their judgements and so on, I simply have to have evidence. It kept me in contact with reality, and I felt comfortable when I had facts to buttress my ideas.

Interviewer: How do you go about choosing your research topic?

Rosenberg: Even from the earliest days, my college days, I was interested in the self-concept and particularly youth. That stayed with me through subsequent years, through the army, and graduate work and so on.

Interviewer: What impact have you hoped that your contribution to survey data analysis would have on social research?

Rosenberg: When I wrote *The Logic of Survey Analysis,* the computers were just coming into play, and in a way the logic was being supplanted by a new mode of data analysis and so on. Basically, I will tell you what I had hoped, and I have no idea whether it was fulfilled or not. When I read social research findings, I found it boring, extremely boring. I found that people presented data, but they didn't think about the meaning of the data. I could see this in study, after study, after study. They didn't think about what caused what. What was the significance of the data? What was the meaning of data? What generalizations could one draw from data?

Not simply presenting data as though it made any difference to have data, but meaning, the importance of meaning. Basically, that is why I wrote *The Logic of Survey Analysis*, to see if I could somehow get across to people how to think with data, think meaningfully with data, and think in an interesting way with data.

Interviewer: In reflecting upon all of your years of research, have you found one project that has been especially enjoyable for you?

Rosenberg: I have alternated between work in methodology and work in research. I have done studies on values; I have done studies of attitudes of various kinds of special populations, and so on. But my interest in self-concept dates back to my college days. What I am forever grateful for, is that it is a topic that is invariably fascinating to me, and there is no danger that I will ever solve it. There are new problems coming up all the time, new ways of looking at things, new issues. It is just an endlessly fascinating subject matter. I guess I did my first study on the self-concept in 1960—that is 30 years ago. Yes, I have done different studies on different populations and so on, but that is one theme that has governed my professional life. I am so grateful I found something that could remain interesting and never get boring.

PAULINE BART, Professor of Sociology, Department of Psychiatry,
University of Illinois, Chicago

"The reality is that the women don't talk about rape or incest until they really trust you, or they are about to leave and the tape recorder is turned off, or if they lived on the north side of Chicago and I would drive them home, on the way home."

Interviewer: What first excited you about social research?

Bart: My need to know, to understand things is a drive, like hunger or thirst or sleep. When something happens and I don't understand it, I feel acutely uncomfortable. And so my dissertation was on depression because my mother had depression and my father said it was my fault. So I wrote a dissertation to find out why middle-aged women became depressed.

Interviewer: What has kept you involved in the field?

Bart: It is basically this drive to understand. People will tell me to do research just because there is money someplace. For example, people will always tell me to do research on alcoholism, and I say, "I don't have any gut feelings for it." And they say, "Well, that means you can be objective." It is so hard to do research—to write and do all of that stuff—to do something that is not really tearing at your soul. Then why bother?

Interviewer: How do you choose one research method over another?

Bart: I should say that in my original research, that is depression, I used the cross-cultural files. The major part of it was looking at hospital records, which drove me crazy. And then somebody said, "Do you want to talk to the women?" And I realized that when I talked to the women at two of the hospitals, that was when I really understood it. Because when you don't actually talk to people, you don't get causal sequences. You don't understand it at the level that I need to understand.

It turns out that I'm very good at it. We were trying to figure out why I am good at it because I was never trained. And apparently, it is because I disclose a lot about myself. And I do this always. And in so doing, it facilitates other people in disclosing.

I know for example in my rape research, (this is a really good story), I had to apply to the National Institute for Mental Health for this. And it kept coming back, and they wanted me to revise it. So a colleague told me to call a very famous methodologist to get him to say that it was O.K. And he told me that I should use random digit dialing. Can you imagine using random digit dialing on that study?—"Oh, have you been raped in the past year?" You get a random sample, but it is worth nothing. I do know men who have done that. The reality is that the women don't talk about rape or incest until they really trust you, or they are about to leave and the tape recorder is turned off, or if they lived on the North side of Chicago, and I would drive them home, on the way home. You don't get that information unless you develop a rapport.

My stuff is usually in the context of discovery. My most important predictive variable I would never have found out if I didn't interview, which was the basic predictor of rape and rape of women was whether their primary reaction was anger or fear. I never thought of that—I never thought women would resist if there were weapons, for example. And this emerged, and I added it.

Interviewer: In dealing with so many sensitive issues, for example, rape and incest, have there been any ethical dilemmas that you had to overcome?

Bart: With my depressed middle-aged women, it was very clear that they were uncomfortable talking about sexuality. And I didn't push it because I wasn't there to pick up the pieces. And, of course, that was also part of the data. I mean, this was in the interview section where I had them look at these TAT-like pictures, these projective pictures, and there was one picture that was very sexual. I also asked them to rank the roles in their lives, and one of them was "being a sexual partner to my husband." And this is embarrassing to them. I just didn't push it.

Interviewer: What do you think has been the greatest challenge as a social researcher?

Bart: I am not a trained therapist. I am a good listener, but I am not a trained therapist. I would sit there with these women who have been raped, and I was the first person who they ever told. It would be like five hours that they would talk with me. I remember at one point wanting to say, "Excuse me, I have to go to the bathroom," while I went and called a therapist friend of mine. But I didn't. I felt terribly responsible.

I am no fun at cocktail parties. Once you see these things, and my students tell me that you can't not see it given the endemic nature of violence against women, it makes life unbearable. Wherever I go, people who know who I am tell me about their rape. It never ends.

I know that if I don't study it, the chances are it will not be studied.

OSWALD HALL, Professor Emeritus, Department of Sociology, University of Toronto

"The greatest challenge of research is how to interview—how to deal with that ever-present nervousness that arises, especially when you, the lowly interviewer, have to interview some person on a much higher social level."

Interviewer: What initially excited you about social research?

Hall: I began back in the Depression, when, in sociology, one of the main concerns was the field of social disorganization. Researchers were interested in poverty, broken families, divorce, desertion, juvenile delinquency, gangs, unemployment, the emergence of prostitution, alcoholism, and mental illness during the Depression. I found myself rejecting that perspective. I thought it would be more interesting to understand social order. What I started to look at is what I called "orderly successful careers"—the orderly going-on of life in major institutions like hospitals, army camps, factories, schools, and business offices. I saw that there was a challenge in the discovery of the adaptation and the adjustment that both persons and organizations made at the major contingencies in social life. It was a wonderful chance at relevant discovery.

Interviewer: What has been your greatest research challenge and how did you deal with it?

Hall: The greatest challenge of research is how to interview—how to deal with that ever-present nervousness that arises, especially when you, the lowly interviewer, have to interview some person on a much higher social level.

As I went on, I discovered that there was a great deal of gratitude on the part of the subjects I interviewed. People in the profession felt two things: (1) They felt proud to be able to give their help to somebody who is active in the field of science, and (2) they also felt that it put them in the position of some importance to be treated in this fashion.

Interviewer: What has been the most horrible research experience that you have ever had?

Hall: One summer I was given a large, unprecedented summer grant to study labor relations in the pulp and paper industry. The employer was distressed about labor turnover, especially among new workers that came over from Europe. I selected a very conscientious graduate student, one who was ambitious to make his mark in sociology, which he later did. I wanted him to do the field, work which involved him traveling to several work camps, and to conduct interviews and later analyze the material. One thing we found was that many of the pulp and paper companies were really heartless regarding their treatment of new Canadians. The company had asked me to see our results before publication and promptly refused to permit publication. There was nothing I could do. The student, of course, was terribly disappointed. The moral of this is to stay away from any research that has strings like that attached.

Interviewer: What ethical dilemmas in social research have you had to overcome?

Hall: The next situation has to do with the unanticipated wound that was suffered by a subject who was interviewed. I was doing some military research for the Canadian army and the problem was how student soldiers learn to be paratroopers. These military students were trained in their regular camp during the basic training and that was followed by a move to some distant airfield for the actual jumps. Before they left, there was a farewell speech by the Colonel. This was a real personal pep talk that he gave to them—to assure them of success on their jump.

When he came to deliver this farewell speech, he invited me to come in. I sat in the back of the room as an observer. And when it was over, he came to me very troubled and said that usually his farewell speech is very carefree, and totally unconscious, and one of the proud aspects of his job that he had to dispose of. He continued to say that "But today, with each second, I was wondering what is Dr. Hall thinking of me as he listens to this lecture. I will never feel so carefree again in giving my speeches to my soldiers."

This isn't a serious ethical dilemma, but a case in which I felt my research was resulting in pain for the other person involved.

Interviewer: Considering that your research has included diverse topics, was there one particular study that you felt had an especially significant impact?

Hall: I did two studies. One of them was called *The Transition from School to Work.* Because we had a lot of research going on about the work world and research about education, I thought I would like to take that little place where the two of them come together, and explore how students make that jump. Then later the Ontario Economic Council asked me and one of my young colleagues to do a study called *The Basic Skills at School and Work: The Study of Albertown.* Of course, this is something that has caught on in a big way in educational systems in both countries, and that is "What are students really getting out of school?"

JAMES COLEMAN, Professor of Sociology and Education, University of Chicago

"Essentially what the research did was show that 'the emperor had no clothes'; it mainly showed something that everybody knew but were afraid to really carry out research on."

Interviewer: What initially excited you about social research?

Coleman: Like a lot of people, I wanted to change the world, that is, I wanted to have some kind of real impact in a direction that I felt was beneficial to society. There were a lot of other things also. The other things were that I had to figure out what was really of a special interest to me, and the thing that was of most interest to me had to do with people. I decided the conjunction between the things that I felt could be of real value to society and things that had to do with people were in sociology.

Interviewer: How about the specific things that you decided to do?

Coleman: Most of the research I have done through my whole career has been in the sociology of education. You can ask the question why I got so interested in this. There are really two reasons. One is because of the fact that I went to several schools when I was young and I saw that the schools really were different in terms of the kind of social system that existed in the school. As a consequence, I was really very much interested in that. I felt that these were the closest things to small social systems—small, independent, not really independent, not really distinct social systems—but little, kind of encapsulated, social systems—that I could find in society, especially high schools. So, I have really been studying high schools ever since.

The second reason comes from the fact that if you look at various kinds of things one might do in sociology, some of them are really just describing the kind of thing that exists. For example, research in social stratification. So you do research in social stratification, and what is the outcome of it? The outcome of it is that you can describe what is going on, describe the stratification system in society. But schools are institutions that are constructed, and, in fact, you can actually change them. There are policies that are directly related to research and so a lot of the work that I have done has been related to policies in schools.

Interviewer: What type of impact did they [your research] have?

Coleman: They had, I think, an impact in changing the terms of the game. That is, in the first work I did for the government called "Equality of Educational Opportunity"— I did that with other people in the U.S. Office of Education, as it was then. Until then equality in schools was really measured by the inputs into education—that is, how much money they spent on education, the education of teachers, and things like that. The work that I did helped to shift the orientation to look at the outputs of education. In other words, no longer just looking at how much money went into schools, but to see whether the school did any good or not.

One of the things that has transpired is that what comes out of schools is not very much related at all to the amount of money that goes into them. So that is where a big transformation occurred. Also, that research was used very extensively in school desegregation court cases which led in the direction of busing in school desegregation.

Interviewer: What was the most horrible research experience you ever had?

Coleman: The most horrible one was when I was attacked by the president of The American Sociological Association [and others]—this was in 1976—for research which showed that busing in large cities produced white flight from those large cities. Now, that was something that nearly everybody except sociologists knew.

Essentially, what the research did was show that "the emperor had no clothes" and it mainly showed something that everybody knew, but they were afraid to really carry out research on. So people really attacked me very, very extensively for that and tried to censor me for the research. So that was an extraordinarily difficult year—when even your friends begin to question what you are doing.

Interviewer: In reflecting upon all of your years of research, has there been any one project which you found especially enjoyable?

Coleman: The most enjoyable research I ever did I think was either *Union Democracy*, the first research I did with Lipset and Trow, or else, *The Adolescent Society*, the research I did on several high schools when I just got out of graduate school. Both of those were really very interesting to me—partly because they weren't just studying individuals, but were studying the functioning of some aspect of the social system. That is what I think sociologists do too little of, and that is what I haven't done enough of through the last 20 years. That's what I am going to begin to do some more of now.

ASSESSMENT QUESTIONS
for *Spotlight on Social Researchers,* Chapter 16

*Name*_____*Date*_____

1. There are some notable differences in the ways in which the social researchers presented in this chapter approach social research. With which researcher do you most closely identify? Whose approach to social research is most different from the approach that you would prefer? Discuss your response.

    Most closely identify:

    Most different:

2. Howard Becker suggests that doing research is a bit like playing Sherlock Holmes, except that in research the researcher is responsible for making up his/her own puzzle. Based on your exposure to research in this class, to what extent do you agree or disagree with Becker's statement? Discuss.

3. Pauline Bart reports that her involvement in research is a response to her "drive to understand." To what extent can you relate to the function of research as a tool for building understanding? Discuss.

4. Develop a set of interview questions similar to the ones presented in this chapter and interview a professor who conducts social research. Take "jotted notes" (brief notes using key words to help you remember the content of the interview). Fill out and review your notes after the interview to answer the following questions:

   a. Whose research style does your professor's style most closely resemble? How?

   b. Whose research style is most different from your professor's style? In what ways?

   c. Whose research interests are closest to your professor's interests? In what ways?

5. Maxine Baca Zinn identifies a term which she calls "conscious partiality" to describe the role of a researcher who is not a completely detached observer. What effect, if any, do you think that conscious partiality would have on the validity and reliability of research? Discuss.

6. James Davis reports that his most rewarding research experience was the General Social Survey (GSS) project which has continued for years and has an impact on our society. What type of research do you think you would find to be most personally rewarding? Why?

Glossary

References

Glossary

Analysis: The comparison and interpretation of empirical evidence.

Applied research: Research designed and conducted from a utilitarian perspective which frequently is used in policy decisions.

Bimodal data distribution: A data distribution in which two values are both frequently observed.

Bivariate data analysis: Statistical analysis of the relationship between two variables, in contrast to univariate data analysis, i.e., the analysis of one variable, and multivariate data analysis, i.e., analysis of the relationship among three or more variables.

Chi-square test: A test of statistical significance most frequently used in cross-tabulations to determine the likelihood that a relationship differs significantly from one which could have occurred by chance.

Closed-ended questions: Questions that provide respondents with a predetermined set of responses from which to choose.

Cluster sampling: A probability sampling technique in which a population is divided into naturally occurring groups from which a random sample of groups, i.e., clusters, are selected.

Codebooks: A researcher's guidebook which lists the questions asked, their response categories, the predetermined protocol for coding decisions, and the location of the data, i.e., the column numbers, in the data file.

Coding: The sorting of responses into a limited number of categories.

Coefficient of reproducibility: The measure of how well a scale represents a true Guttman scale, i.e., the percentage of correct responses that could be reproduced simply by knowing the scale scores.

Conceptualization: The development and articulation of the meaning of an abstract concept.

Construct validity: A characteristic of an indicator derived from an evaluation of an operational definition as to whether the findings are consistent with the theoretical argument and prior research findings.

Content analysis: A research method in which information from written documents, e.g., newspapers and legal records, or visual media, e.g., television shows and motion pictures, is systematically categorized and counted.

Content validity: A characteristic of an indicator derived from the subjective evaluation by the researcher as to whether the operational definition represents all of the potential aspects of an abstract concept.

Control condition: In experimental research, subjects are assigned to control and experimental groups in order to test the effect of an independent variable. The control group is not subjected to the test condition, i.e., the independent variable, while the experimental group is.

Control variables: Variables whose values are held constant in a statistical analysis or in all conditions of an experiment.

Convenience sample: A non-probability sample in which the researcher selects respondents because of the accessibility of the respondents (for example, college students who participate in surveys in their psychology courses).

Data: Observations collected as part of a research project.

Database: A compilation of information which frequently is stored on computer tapes or disks.

Dependent variable: The variable in a causal relationship which the researcher is attempting to explain.

Descriptive research: A study whose purpose is to define and characterize human behavior, societies, events, or other social phenomenon.

Empirical method: A scientific research approach which requires direct or indirect observations as evidence.

Ethnographic research: The study of natural populations through non-invasive techniques, e.g., participation and observation.

Evaluation research: Research which either designs, monitors the implementation, or measures the effectiveness of social programs or policies.

Experimentation: A research method in which subjects are first assigned to control and test groups, and then one or more variables are either introduced or manipulated in the test group, but not in the control group. Through the use of experimentation, researchers are able to control, i.e., hold at a constant value, many extraneous variables, and therefore, are better able to eliminate alternative explanations for their research findings than is possible with other research strategies.

Explanatory research: A study whose purpose is to explain a relationship between two or more variables.

Exploratory research: A study whose purpose is to investigate and describe behaviors, societies, events, and other social phenomenon about which little is known.

Face validity: A characteristic of an indicator derived from the subjective evaluation by the researcher as to whether the operational definition represents the intended concept.

Field notes: Detailed accounts of observations made in natural settings.

Field setting: The natural environment in which behaviors occur.

Frequency distribution: A listing of the number of cases observed in each value of a variable.

Generalizability: The extent to which research findings can be extended or applied to other groups of people, locations or periods of times.

Guttman scale: An ordered arrangement of items in terms of their relative strength. Guttman scales summarize data for statistical analysis.

Hypothesis: A testable statement or claim predicting a relationship between two or more variables.

Independent variable: The variable in a causal relationship which the researcher predicts will influence or affect the dependent variable.

Indicator: An observation that is assumed by the researcher to be representative of an abstract concept. For example, pre-tax income might be an indicator of the concept "social class."

Instrumentation: The stage of research in which the data collection tools, such as questionnaires or interview guides are developed.

Interaction: The portion of the combined effect of two or more independent variable which differs from the effects of the individual variables. For example, adult children who live further away from their parents may visit their parents less often than adult children who live nearby, but the effect of distance on contact will be much greater for adult children with low-incomes than for affluent adult children.

Interview: a data collection method in which individuals are asked a series of questions.

Interview schedule: A survey instrument consisting of instructions for the interviewer, carefully ordered questions, and predetermined response choices for the closed-ended questions.

Longitudinal survey design: A method of collecting survey data at different intervals over an extended period of time.

Matching: The technique for assigning subjects to control and treatment groups in which each subject is matched on characteristics thought to be related to the dependent variable with a subject in the other group.

Measurement: The process of assigning numbers or symbols to units of analysis in order to describe abstract concepts in terms of measurable indicators.

Measures: The specific indicators or items that represent the abstract concepts of concern to social researchers.

Methodology: A research strategy, e.g., experiment, survey, field research, and content analysis.

Multiple regression: A statistical method of data analysis which allows the researcher to determine the simultaneous effects of two or more variables on a dependent variable.

Multistage cluster sample: A sample which is drawn through more than one step and involves moving from large clusters of the population to smaller and smaller clusters, e.g., first drawing a sample of grade schools from among the various school districts across the country, then drawing a sample of fifth grade classrooms from the pre-selected grade schools, and finally drawing a sample of fifth graders from the pre-selected classrooms.

Multivariate data analysis: The statistical analysis of the simultaneous relationship among three or more variables, in contrast to univariate data analysis, i.e., the statistical analysis of one variable, and bivariate data analysis, i.e., the analysis of the relationship between two variables.

Nominal definition: Definitions which describe a phenomenon, but are too abstract for empirical testing.

Non-probability sample: A sample that is not selected randomly, i.e., each unit in the population did not have an equal chance of being included in the sample.

Non-random selection: Any process in which every unit in the population does not have an equal chance of being included in the sample.

Observational design: A method of collecting data in which the researcher directly witnesses the behavior.

Open-ended questions: Questions that require respondents to answer in their own words.

Operational definition: Definitions which describe the phenomenon in terms of observable and measurable characteristics.

Operationalization: The detailed description of the research procedures necessary to ensure consistent findings.

Ordinal measurement: The categorization of data into mutually exclusive and ranked groupings.

Participant observation: A research method in which the researcher participates in the ongoing activities of the individuals or setting being studied.

Population: All of the possible cases in a predetermined grouping of individuals, societies, or events.

Posttest: A measure which occurs after the experimental treatment occurs.

Predictive validity: A characteristic of an indicator derived from a criterion-related evaluation as to whether an operational definition represents a concept. Predictive validity utilizes a measure to represent an individual's performance or standing in the future, e.g., the use of SAT-scores or high school grades to predict students' performance in college.

Pretest: A measure which occurs before the experimental treatment occurs.

Probability sample: A sample in which each unit in the population of interest had an equal chance of being included in the sample.

Qualitative research: Research which features interpretive description rather than statistics.

Quantitative research: Research which relies on complex statistics derived through objective methods of data collection and interpretation.

Quasi-experiment: a research method that approximates experimental control in a natural setting. Quasi-experiments often may lack all of the features of a true experiment, e.g., randomization.

Questionnaire: A survey instrument which consists of a set of written questions for respondents to complete.

Quota sample: A non-probability sample which involves dividing the population into categories from which a predetermined number of cases are selected for inclusion in the sample.

Random assignment: The technique for assigning subjects to control and treatment groups in which each subject has an equal chance of being assigned to either group. Also referred to as randomization.

Random sample: See *Simple random sample.*

Random selection: A process that provides each unit in the population of interest an equal opportunity of being included in the sample.

Ratio measurement: The highest level of measurement, i.e., the categorization of data which have an absolute zero point into mutually exclusive, systematically ranked, and equally spaced groupings.

Reliability: The degree to which a measure yields consistent findings each time it is employed.

Research ethics: The standards of responsible and moral behavior required by researchers for the protection of the participants and the general public.

Respondents: The individuals from whom information is collected in survey research.

Response bias: Systematic error in respondents' answers which occurs because of the order or content of the survey questions. For example, a respondent may provide an insincere answer because the response is considered socially desirable.

RFP: "Request for Proposal" developed by a funding agency in order to solicit research proposals which are applicable to the funding agency's interest. For example, a job training program might issue an RFP to seek research proposals which would help them better understand the factors which contribute to job retention among recently employed individuals.

Sample: A subset of cases selected from the population of interest.

Sampling bias: Systematic error in a sample as a result of problems associated with the sampling frame or data collection, e.g., the use of the telephone directory as a sampling frame or only sampling during the daytime.

Sampling frame: A listing of all the units of a population from which a sample may be selected.

Scientific method: A systematic research technique which posits and tests hypotheses through a series of clear and consistent steps in order to maximize objectivity in the collection and interpretation of data.

Selection bias: Error which occurs when all of the units in a population do not have an equal chance of being included in the sample or when cases are not randomly assigned in an experiment.

Simple random sample: A probability sample in which each unit in the population of interest has an equal chance of being selected for the sample.

Snowball sample: A non-probability sample in which the initial respondents for the study refer the researcher to other similar respondents. Snowball sampling is most frequently used in field research on topics that might be illegal, personal, or controversial, e.g., studies of white-collar crime or adultery.

Stratified random sample: A probability sample in which the population is divided into strata, and cases from each stratum are randomly selected for inclusion in the sample.

Structured interview: An interview in which all the questions are predetermined and each respondent is asked the questions in the same order.

Study design: A detailed plan which describes how the research will be conducted.

Survey instrument: The interview schedule or questionnaire used in survey research.

Survey research: A data collection method in which information is collected from individuals either by personal interviews or through written questionnaires.

Systematic sample: A probability sample in which cases for study are selected by including those units that appear in the sampling frame after a random start and at a predetermined interval, e.g., beginning with the tenth student listed in the University Registrar's records and including every fiftieth student whose name appears on the list after that.

Test condition: In experimental research, subjects are assigned to control and experimental groups in order to test the effect of an independent variable. The experimental group is subjected to the test condition, i.e., the independent variable, while the control group is not.

Testing effect: A potential bias or error which can occur when a measure is administered more than once to the same group or individual.

Test of statistical significance: A statistical procedure that indicates the likelihood that the finding of a difference between groups could have occurred by chance.

Units of analysis: The specific objects, entities, or events about which the researcher collects and analyzes information.

Univariate data analysis: Statistical analysis of one variable, in contrast to bivariate data analysis, i.e., the analysis of the relationship between two variables, and multivariate data analysis, i.e., analysis of the relationship among three or more variables.

Unobtrusive methods: Research techniques in which the units of analysis are not aware that they are being studied, for example, analysis of historical materials or observations of a subject's behavior without his or her knowledge.

Unstructured interview: A non-standardized interview in which each respondent may be asked different questions. Unstructured interviews are often used when a researcher is gathering preliminary information about the topic or question.

Validity: The degree to which a measure represents the abstract concept it is intended to estimate.

References

Chapter 1

Allport, Gordon W. and Leo Postman. 1947. *The Psychology of Rumor.* New York: Holt.

Crawley, Donna and Martha Ecker. 1990. "Integrating Issues of Gender, Race, and Ethnicity into Experimental Psychology and Other Social Science Methodology Courses." *Women's Studies Quarterly 1 & 2*: 102-117.

Fox, Mary Frank and Sharlene Hesse-Biber. 1984. *Women at Work.* Mountain View, CA: Mayfield.

Kelman, Herbert C. 1968. *A Time to Speak: On Human Values and Social Research.* San Francisco: Jossey Bass Inc.

Penn, Elizabeth M. 1986. "The Theater of Work: How Some Youth Get Better Parts." In K. M. Borman & J. Reisman (Eds.), *Becoming A Worker* (pp. 201-217). Norwood, NJ: Ablex.

Chapter 2

Reisman, Jane, Anderson, Dana, Marchetti, Veeda, Bullinger, Michele, Roe, Kaaren, and Suzanne Sheperd. 1987. *Study of Mentally-Disabled Street People in Downtown Tacoma.* Tacoma, Washington: Division of Social Sciences, Pacific Lutheran University, January.

Snow, David A., Baker, Susan G., Anderson, Leon, and Michael Martin. 1986. "The Myth of Pervasive Mental Illness among the Homeless," *Social Problems, 33 (5)*: 407-423, June.

Chapter 3

Blumstein, Philip and Pepper Schwartz. 1983. *American Couples: Money, Work, Sex.* New York: William Morrow and Co.

Fishman, Pamela, M. 1990. "Women's Work in Interaction," in John W. Heeren and Marylee Mason (Eds.), *Sociology: Windows on Society.* Los Angeles: Roxbury Publishing Co.

Rank, Mark R. 1989. "Fertility among Women on Welfare: Incidence and Determinants," *American Sociological Review, 54*: 296-304, April.

Chapter 4

Rubin, Lillian B. 1983. *Intimate Strangers: Men and Women Together.* New York: Harper & Row.

Wellman, David T. 1977. *Portraits of White Racism.* Cambridge: Cambridge University Press.

Maccoby, Eleanor E., & Jacklin, Carolyn N. 1974. *The Psychology of Sex Differences.* Stanford, CA: Stanford University Press.

Lips, Hilary M. 1988. *Sex and Gender: An Introduction.* Mountain View, CA: Mayfield Publishing Co.

Condry, J. & Ross, D. 1985. "Sex and Aggression: The Influence of Gender Label on the Perception of Aggression in Children." *Child Development, 56*: 225-233.

Chapter 5

Sudnow, David. 1967. *Passing On: The Social Organization of Dying.* Englewood Cliffs, NJ: Prentice-Hall.

Chapter 6

Ferraro, Kathleen J. and John M. Johnson. 1983. "How Women Experience Battering: The Process of Victimization," *Social Problems, 30 (3):* 325-339, February.

Powell, Lindsay. Personal communication.

Chapter 7

Cannon, Lynn Weber, Higginbotham, Elizabeth, and Marianne L.A. Leung. 1988. "Race and Class Bias in Qualitative Research on Women." *Gender & Society 2* (4): 449-462.

Gilbert, G. Nigel. 1981. *SAMP: Survey Sampling Instructor's Guide.* Conduit, Iowa City, Iowa.

Chapter 8

Cherlin, Andrew J., Furstenberg, Frank F. Jr., Chase-Lansdale, Linsay, Kiernan, Kathleen E., Robins, Phillip K., Morrison, Donna Ruane, and Julien O. Teitler. 1991. "Longitudinal Studies of Effects of Divorce on Children in Great Britain and the United States." *Science 252*: 1386-1389.

Chapter 9

Myerhoff, Barbara. 1978. *Number Our Days.* New York: Simon and Schuster, A Touchstone Book.

Chapter 10

Shaver, K.G. 1970. "Defensive Attribution: Effects of Severity and Relevance on the Responsibility Assigned for an Accident." *Journal of Personality and Social Psychology 14*: 101-113.

Linz, Daniel, Donnerstein, Edward, Land, Kenneth C., McCall, Patricia L., Scott, Joseph, Bradley, J. Shafer, Klein, Lee J., and Larry Lance. 1991. "Estimating Community Standards: The Use of Social Science Evidence in an Obscenity Prosecution." *Public Opinion Quarterly 55*: 80-112.

Lubomski, Lisa, Anderson, Dana D., Wienhold, Maria, and Orme, Matthew. 1987. "Defensive Attributions of Rape When the Victim is Male Versus Female," Paper presented at the Western Psychological Association Annual Meeting, San Francisco, CA.

Chapter 11

Hendershott, Anne, Stephen Norland, Douglas Eichar, Jack Powell. 1991. "The Impact of Interdistrict Cooperative Learning on the Racial Attitudes of Elementary School Students." *Sociological Practice Review 2*: 95-103.

Koslin, Sandra, Marianne Amarel and Nancy Ames. 1968. "A Distance Measure of Racial Attitudes in Primary Grade Children." *Psychology in the Schools 6*: 382-385.

Koslin, Sandra, Bertram Koslin and Richard Pergament. 1972. "Classroom Balance and Student Interracial Attitudes." *Sociology of Education 45*: 386-407.

Little, Craig B. "Sociological Moonlighting: Practical Advice About Consulting for Local Government." *Sociological Practice Review 2* (3): 217-223.

Katz, Phyllis A. 1976. "The Acquisition of Racial Attitudes in Children." In P. Katz (Ed.), *Toward the Elimination of Racism*. New York: Pergamon Press.

Newman, Many, Marsha Liss and Felicia Sherman. 1983. "Ethnic Awareness in Children: Not a Unitary Concept." *Journal of Genetic Psychology 143*: 103-112.

Chapter 12

Demetrulias, Diana Mayer and Nina Ribak Rosenthal. 1985. "Discrimination Against Females and Minorities in Microcomputer Advertising." *Computers and the Social Sciences 1*:91-95.

Genovese, Eugene D. 1986. "The Myth of the Absent Family." In Robert Staples (Ed.), *The Black Family: Essays and Studies*, Third Edition (pp. 29-34). Belmont, CA: Wadsworth Publishing Co.

Chapter 13

Siegel, Karolynn and Beatrice J. Krauss. 1991. "Living with HIV Infection: Adaptive Tasks of Seropositive Gay Men," *The Journal of Health and Social Behavior, 32* (1): 17-32, March.

Chapter 14

Coleman, James William. 1989. *The Criminal Elite: The Sociology of White Collar Crime*. New York: St. Martin's Press.

National Center for Health Statistics. 1991. "Annual Summary of Births, Marriages, Divorces, and Deaths: United States, 1990." Monthly vital statistics report, 39, 13, Hyattsville, Maryland, Public Health Service.

Poston, Dudley L. Jr. and Falbo, Toni. 1990. "Academic Performance and Personality Traits of Chinese Children: 'Onlies' versus Others." *American Journal of Sociology 96* (2): 443-51.

Roethlisberger, Fred J. and William J. Dickson. 1939. *Management and the Worker*. Cambridge, MA: Harvard University Press.

Roy, Donald. 1952. "Quota Restriction and Goldbricking in a Machine Shop." *American Journal of Sociology 57* (5): 422-42.

U.S. Special Commission on Aging. 1989. *Aging America: Trends and Projections—1987-88 Edition*. U.S. Department of Health and Human Services.

Vaz, Edmund W. 1984. "Institutionalized Stealing Among Big-City Taxi Drivers." In A. Wipper (Ed.), *The Sociology of Work: Papers in Honor of Oswald Hall* (pp. 75-91). Ottawa, Canada: Carleton University Press.

Chapter 15

Haensly, Patricia, Ann Lupkowski, James McNamara. 1987. "The Chart Essay: A Strategy for Communicating Research Findings to Policymakers and Practitioners," *Educational Evaluation and Policy Analysis, 9,* (1): 63-75, Spring.

McNamara, James & the EPSY Survey Research Group. 1983. *National Survey of Former TAMU College of Education on Graduate Students: A Chart Essay Presented to the College of Education Committee on Follow-up of Graduates and Evaluation of Teacher Education Programs*. College Station: Texas A&M University. February.

McNamara, James, Patricia Haensly, and Ann Lupkowski, and E.P. Edlind. 1985. *The Role of Extracurricular Activities in High School Education: A Chart Essay on Survey Findings*. College Station: Texas A&M University. (ERIC Document Reproduction Service No. ED 268 712)

Washington Child Health Research and Policy Group. 1991. *The State of Washington's Children. Summary Report*, June.